A GUIDE
DEVON DIALECT

formerly entitled

A Dictionary of Devon Dialect

JOHN DOWNES

TABB HOUSE
Padstow

First published 1986
Second Edition 1998
Tabb House, 7 Church Street, Padstow
Cornwall, PL28 8BG

ISBN 1 873951 23 X

British Library Cataloguing-in-Publication Data:
A catalogue record of this title is available from the British Library.

Printed and bound by T.J. International, Padstow, Cornwall

*   *   *

ACKNOWLEDGEMENTS

I acknowledge with gratitude the help and encouragement I
have continued to receive from E.W.Martin Esq., FR Hist.S,
and from the many readers who have been good enough to
write to me with suggestions and comment. Notwithstanding
their assistance, I still must take responsibility for any errors
or omissions in this book.

Woolsfardisworthy   John Downes

Bideford   1998

CONTENTS

FOREWORD

THIS book was originally published in 1986 as *A Dictionary of Devon Dialect*, but experience has shown that the title was misleading and it was never intended to be an exhaustive dictionary. It is hoped that the title of the new edition will be seen as more appropriate.

It has been suggested that I should expand the guide to include some of the words that appear in certain other publications, but in my opinion many such words are archaic and of historical interest only and others are of doubtful value as examples of dialect. Instead, I have tried to verify every word listed in this edition, having *personally* heard most of them in the everyday speech of those Devonians who are still not ashamed to use their native tongue.

Had it not been for Eric Partridge, I doubt if I would ever have attempted to write this book. I will introduce it by quoting from his book *Usage and Abusage: A Guide to Good English*.

It is to be hoped that dialect-speakers will not be shamed out of their words, phrases, and pronunciations by 'cultured' visitors, by near-visioned teachers, by B.B.C. 'experts'. The influence of 'education' is already visible in the weakening of the local pronunciation of Cirencester (Sissiter), Bodiam (Bodjum), Daventry (Danetree), Yealm (Yam): it is time that the curb and snaffle of good sense should put a check to the nefarious teaching of the unimaginatively genteel. Country people are too modest. They must sturdily resist the insidious approaches of their 'betters'. They should boldly preserve the traditional pronunciations.

1

A BACKGROUND TO DIALECT

BETWEEN 1950 and 1962 a survey of English dialects was made by the Department of English Language and Medieval English Literature at Leeds University. Planned in 1946, this survey grew from a proposal made by Professor Dieth of the University of Zurich that he and Professor Harold Orton of Leeds should together compile a 'linguistic atlas' of England. Unfortunately, Professor Dieth died in 1956 before the work was completed.

The Leeds Survey, which must be respected by all scholars of the English language, consists of twelve volumes, covers all English dialects and is a very detailed and academic work. However, it was clearly never intended for the general reader and my aim has simply been to provide a book that is.

While there has long been an interest in dialect, there is considerable misunderstanding about what the word means. Many people seem to confuse it with regional accent and when they call for dialect to be preserved or even taught in schools, they are probably thinking more of regional accents than of dialect.

That these accents are a part of dialect is unarguable, but there are many people who speak with regional accents who know few true dialect words, and the number of people who use genuine dialect in normal conversation is decreasing and will continue to decrease.

The definition of dialect is interesting and complex. The OED says that dialect is:

Manner of speaking, language, speech; esp. one peculiar to an

1

individual or class; phraseology, idiom . . . A variety of speech differing from the standard language; a provincial method of speech.

This definition covers a great deal of ground, but I believe that dialect contains at least six different ingredients which mix together to make a diverse and fascinating whole. They are:

    a. local pronunciation
    b. regional accent (related to pronunciation)
    c. grammatical construction that differs from what is generally accepted as being correct
    d. unusual use of standard words
    e. the deliberate or accidental misuse of standard words
    f. the use of archaic words in normal conversation.

Evidence suggest that regional dialects were once widely spoken by all social classes. Trevelyan says that in Queen Anne's time the country squire spoke in a broad provincial dialect and was only distinguished from the yeoman by the respect paid to him by others. This situation did not last.

During the seventeenth and eighteenth centuries there appears to have been a widespread desire to purify languages. Academics had for a long time regarded Latin as being the only model for language and literature and many had attempted to refine English on Latin lines. It is obvious that standardisation of both grammar and spelling was highly desirable for the spelling of the same words often differed from line to line. Edward VI's prayerbook, introduced in 1549 but still in daily use in the first half of the seventeenth century, provides many examples:

O ye waters that be aboue the fyrmamente, speake good of the *Lorde* prayse hym, and set hym up for euer
O all ye powers of the Lord, speake good of the *Lord* . . .

In the prayer-book the words *Catholic faith* are spelled *Catholyke fayth* in one line and, three lines later, *Catholike faith*. Even a simple word like *him* varied, being spelled as it is now in one line and *hym* in the next. There was a desire for uniformity, but no standard to which one could refer.

Shakespeare could not decide how to spell even his own name. It ranged from *Chacksper* to *Shaxpere*, from *Shakespere* or *Shakespeyre* to *Schakespeir* and even *Schakspere*, and there were other variations. He invented words of his own; some survive only in his works and have not been used by anyone else. But some of the words which he coined have become part of the English language and include such commonplace words as *accommodation, dislocate, premeditate* and *submerge*. Another word which he almost certainly invented is *auspicious* (or rather, *inauspicious,*) and this word seems to have arrived on the stage when Romeo says, just before he commits suicide,

> . . . here, will I remain
> With worms that are thy chambermaids: O here
> Will I set up my everlasting rest;
> And shake the yoke of *inauspicious* stars
> From this world-wearied flesh. Eyes, look
> your last! . . .

He obtained the word from the Latin *auspex* (someone who looked for omens in the flight of birds).

The first English dictionary I know of was a book of 120 pages written by Robert Cawdrey in 1604 called *The Table Alphabeticall of Hard Words*. This was followed in 1616, the year of Shakespeare's death, by John Bullokar's *English Expositor*, and a book called *A Guide Into Tongues* appeared in 1617.

Cockeram published his *English Dictionarie: or an Interpreter of Hard English Words* in 1623, but this, like earlier works, was merely a list of difficult words with no attempt to provide etymology or examples of usage.

In 1658 Milton's nephew Edward Phillips produced a book

called *A New World of English Words*. This was followed in
1721 by the publication of Bailey's *Universal Etymological
English Dictionary* but even the improved edition, which was
not published until 1736, was inferior to works produced on
their respective languages by academies in Italy and in France.

As I have implied, the desire to codify and purify language
was not confined to England, and the *Accademia della Crusca*
had been founded as long ago as 1582 to purify the Italian
language. In 1635 Cardinal Richelieu had been responsible for
the foundation of a society which came to be known as the
Académie Français, the function of which was to give definitive
rulings on the French language.

In 1712 Jonathan Swift addressed a letter to the Earl of
Oxford, the Lord Treasurer of England, proposing that certain
suitable persons should assemble to produce rules to codify the
English language.

Nothing came of this, principally because of the death of
Queen Anne, for the Lord Treasurer had hoped to use his
influence with the Queen to obtain funds from which the cost
could be met. Swift had, in effect, proposed the formation of an
academy similar to those already existing in Italy and in France,
but many, including Dr Johnson, opposed it. Johnson hoped that
'the spirit of English liberty' would hinder or destroy the
establishment of such an institution. When his own dictionary
was published in 1755 he established a standard that remained
unchallenged for almost one hundred years.

As this seventeenth and eighteenth century cultural revolution
was taking place the social structure of the countryside was
undergoing change. Land values almost doubled between 1700
and 1790 and more and more land was brought into cultivation.
Better farming methods were introduced and experiments were
made with crop rotation. These new methods required land to be
enclosed and the procedure used to achieve this was usually by
an Act of Parliament, seldom by voluntary agreement.

Between 1760 and 1801 more than 1,300 Enclosure Acts
were passed, and then a General Enclosure Act was introduced

to make the process simpler. By 1820 almost 1,000 more acts were passed, transforming not only the appearance of the countryside but the lives of the rural working classes. It took away the independence of many smallholders who had kept their livestock on common land. An anonymous writer in the *Tickler Magazine* said on February 1st, 1821,

> The fault is great in man or woman
> Who steals a goose from off a common;
> But what can plead that man's excuse
> Who steals a common from the goose?

When enclosed land became private property the formerly independent small farmer had no option but to become a farm labourer or go to seek work in the growing industrial towns.

Europe had been at war for many years and the transition to peace brought with it many problems. In 1825 William Cobbett claimed that taxation, the National Debt, the issue of paper money, and what he delighted to call 'The Thing'(meaning the system of Government which he so deplored), had contributed towards turning farm workers into paupers and separating them from the farmers and yeomen.

Cobbett claimed that it cost less to pay farm workers money and to house them in cottages than it had cost to board them in the farmer's own house. He speaks of this 'accursed system' which turned farmers into a 'species of mock gentlefolk, while it has ground the labourers down into real slaves.' He said that the squire's father

. . . used to, I dare say, sit at the head of the oak table along with his men, say grace with them, and cut up the meat and the pudding. He might take a cup of strong beer to himself when they have none; but that was pretty nearly all the difference in their manner of living . . .

As a direct result of these social changes, it became the fashion for farmers and the new rural gentry to send their children away to school where they were taught to 'speak properly' and to read and learn the classics. The gap between the ploughboy and the farmer's son widened, and there developed a difference in their mode of speech. Ernest Martin says in his book *The Secret People* that the enclosures so upset the balance of rural life that many farmers found it difficult to determine their place in society. Some aped the squire simply because they no longer knew where they belonged.

A farmer in Berkshire, quoted by Lord Ernle, expressed the dominant social attitudes of two periods of village life:

1743	1843
Man, to the plough:	Man, Tally Ho!
Wife, to the cow;	Miss, Piano,
Girl, to the yarn;	Wife, Silk and Satin,
Boy, to the Barn;	Boy, Greek and Latin
And your Rent will	And you'll all be
be netted	Gazetted.

There is plenty of other evidence in contemporary literature of these changes and in *Persuasion* Jane Austen said:

... the Musgroves, like their houses, were in a state of alteration, perhaps improvement. The father and mother were in the old English style and the young people in the new. Mr and Mrs Musgrove were a very good sort of people; friendly and hospitable, not much educated, and not at all elegant ... [their daughters] had brought from a school at Exeter all the usual stock of accomplishments, and were now, like thousands of other young ladies, living to be fashionable ...

This upheaval in the pattern of country life and speech continued uninterrupted because until the introduction of the first Education Act in 1870 very few children of labourers received any education. They learned, as their fathers had learned before them, by word of mouth.

It was during this period that a few educated persons became interested in the traditional speech of the County, and although the earliest example of Devon dialect recorded in writing is probably *The Exmoor Scolding and Courtship*, published in 1746, most interest seems to have come during the nineteenth century. In the early 1800s Mrs Palmer, a sister of Sir Joshua Reynolds, wrote a little story in Devon dialect. This was edited and published by her daughter, Mrs Gwatkin of Great Torrington, in 1839.

In 1866 Sir John Bowring, who had become President of the Devonshire Association for the Advancement of Science, Literature and Art in 1862, presented a paper at Tavistock on the subject of dialect, saying

It is not a hazardous prophecy to announce that in a few generations no language but English, and that, a grammatical English, will be spoken throughout the British Territories. The old British is dead, the Gaelic will perish next, then the Welsh and last, probably Erse, or Irish, and then our Mother tongue, emphatically English, will be the sole sovereign over the whole dominions of our written and spoken literature. Education and fashion will cause the diversities of colloquial idioms to disappear . . .

Sir John then said:

Half a century ago, the county of a country gentleman was easily discoverable wherever he went; 'You are a Devonshire, a Yorkshire, a Kentishman' frequently larded the conversation . . .

In 1875 Frederick Thomas Elworthy, who became President of the Devonshire Association in 1906, read a paper before the Philological Society entitled 'The Dialect of West Somerset'. Elworthy said that the claim that the last trace of Briton, Saxon, and Dane would soon be swept out of the land by railways, telegraphs, machinery, and steam was highly coloured.

He believed that the introduction of modern improvements and the advance of science had far less effect on dialect than was generally supposed by those whose acquaintance with dialect was confined, in the most part, to what others had written. One cannot help wondering what he would have thought of the effects of radio and television. Nevertheless he was right, and one must turn again to Dr Johnson for the real reason. He said in the preface to his dictionary:

As language was at its beginning merely oral, all words of necessary or common use were spoken before they were written; and while they were unfixed by any visible signs, must have been spoken with great diversity, as we now observe those who cannot read to catch sounds imperfectly and utter them negligently. When this wild and barbarous jargon was first reduced to an alphabet, every penman endeavoured to express, as he could, the sounds which he was accustomed to pronounce or to receive, and vitiated in writing such words as were already vitiated in speech . . . from this uncertain pronunciation arise in great part the various dialects of the same country, which will always be observed to grow fewer, and less different, as books are multiplied . . .

Dialect is not being destroyed or killed. It is simply dying of old age.

This is true of many things but while dialect is not an artifact that can be encased in plastic or preserved in a museum, unless it is recorded it will, sooner or later, be lost for ever.

This was the view of the Devonshire Association when in 1877 it appointed a committee to record what it called 'verbal provincialisms'. The regulations of that committee are not without interest. Members were urged

To regard the following as Devonshire Provincialisms if used by a speaker or writer within Devonshire, irrespective of their being, or not being, used elsewhere:

(a) Every word not occurring in a good English dictionary of the present day.

(b) Every word which, though occurring in any good English dictionary of the present day, is used in a sense differing from any definition used in such a dictionary.

(c) Every provincial pronunciation of such a word which is not in itself a provincialism.

(d) Every provincial phrase or expression.

(e) Every provincial name of an animal, vegetable or other object.

There were ten regulations that required members to note where each provincialism was heard, or seen in writing, and to accept nothing second-hand. Members were required to state the sex, occupation, residence, birth-place, and age of the person using the provincialism.

The terms of reference suggest that dialect was already being treated as something of a curiosity, the language of creatures living in a strange etymological zoo rather than as a living language, which, until relatively recently, had been in general use.

The committee dispersed in 1923 but since then the Devonshire Association has appointed a Recorder of Dialect whose report appears in the annual transactions of the Association. When the first recorder was appointed, the rules and regulations were slightly modified but they remain substantially the same as the original ones.

R. Pearse Chope, who became the President of the Devonshire Assocation in 1926, read a paper before it in July 1891 that was later published under the title of *The Dialect of Hartland, Devonshire*. The paper was originally prepared as a commentary on Elworthy's *The West Somerset Word Book*. Chope seems to have accepted that education and 'progress' was responsible for the gradual disappearance of dialect:

. . . it is obvious that the old words are retained longest where the progress is slowest; that is in those places which are furthest from the railways, because board schools and newspapers are now common to all.

Bideford is no longer connected with London by the railway and Hartland is now further from the railway than it was in 1891, but the trains have been replaced by motor cars which, with radio and television, bring 'progress' to all.

But although Bowring and Elworthy spoke of the approaching death of dialect and whilst a committee was created in 1877 to record dialect before it disappeared completely, it is still spoken by many people. Nevertheless, it is still on its way out and one must ask why.

'What' demanded Dr Johnson, 'makes a word obsolete more than general agreement to forbear it?'

Dialect is disappearing because most people do not want to use it. But despite this, there is a genuine interest in dialect for its own sake, perhaps a nostalgia for the speech of the past and a reluctance to see yet another milestone of social history disappear for ever.

Sadly, mock dialect is now used to indicate the whereabouts of the public bar or the lavatories with signs like YER TIZ or UP YER. This sort of thing, plus what has so aptly been called on radio and television the Mummerset accent, and articles in magazines and newspapers which pretend to be dialect (but which are in fact stories written to convey to the uninitiated, the impression of dialect), is all that many people know, or care, about the dying language of our county.

2

ACCENT AND PRONUNCIATION

NO matter what method is used, it is not easy to record 'accent' in writing. It is even more difficult to differentiate between accent and pronunciation. Was it, for example, pronunciation or accent which caused the downfall of the Ephraimites at the passage of Jordan? 'Say now Shibboleth: and he said Sibboleth: for he could not frame to pronounce it right' (Judges XII. v.6) is surely one of the earliest references to this complex subject.

Most people can without difficulty recognise a so-called American accent, or a North Country or Westcountry accent. Americans even refer to a 'British' accent but probably mean what used to be called an Oxford accent or one of the many regional accents which proclaim the speaker to be British.

In Shaw's *Pygmalion* Professor Higgins, by listening to a person speak, is able to say where in London, within a few streets, the speaker comes from. While this is far-fetched, accents can be used to identify a speaker's origins. The accent of a Bostonian differs from that of a Texan, that of a Lancastrian from that of a man from York, and so to the informed ear the accent of a Devonian may easily be distinguished from that of a Cornishman.

Even within the county, which is very large, accent and pronunciation differ considerably. Natives of Appledore, for example have a most distinctive accent. What then *is* accent? It is a subtle combination of pronunciation, tone, and voice production. It has an almost musical quality and can range from a soft burr-like sound to a shrill shriek. One lady, who has un-wittingly over the years provided me with much material for this book, has a voice which might shatter glasses at twenty paces!

11

While English is not a tonal language, as is Cantonese, the tone, (or tune?) cannot be ignored, and if accent is accepted as being the equivalent to the tune of a language then most Devonians know the tune but many have forgotten, or have never learned, the words.

Anyone may learn the words but it is difficult to learn the tune and foreigners, even local foreigners like me, who attempt to speak in dialect by using the words *and* the accent can easily cause amusement or even give offence when local people think that they are being mocked. This is regrettable because not only does one not want to give offence, but it drives true dialect deeper and deeper underground.

We now come to a most important point; Bowring referred to mispronunciation, and fell into what I consider to be the arrogance of claiming that dialectal pronunciation is merely a quaint way of pronouncing standard English. I am certain that this is the wrong approach. Many educated and cultured people use variations of pronunciation which have nothing to do with their regional origins. The simple word *off*, which, to most, rhymes with *toff*, is frequently pronounced as if it were spelled *orf*. Similarly the word *golf* is often pronounced *goff*. Which of these is the correct pronunciation? There is much evidence to suggest that pronunciation changes with the times and, for example, in the early 1980s the use of the glottal stop in the speech of educated people was regarded as a phenomenon, but nowadays it tends to be widespread in all social classes. One must also consider and wonder at the arrival of the long A which is affected by many young persons. Simple words like *black*, *that*, *cat* and *rat* appear to have developed an extra long vowel sound, perhaps by a swing of a linguistic pendulum from the old fashioned prissy speech which caused these words to become *bleck*, *thet*, *ket* and *ret*?

Reference to eighteenth-century poetry indicates that some words may once have been pronounced in a very different way. There are many examples of this. Alexander Pope (1688-1744) used words which in present-day English no longer rhyme:

> Good-nature and good sense must ever join;
> To err is human, to forgive divine.

If Pope really pronounced *join* as *jine*, then this is preserved in Devon dialect. This quotation interested me a great deal and I looked for and found some more. Pope again:

> Whose herds with milk, whose fields with bread,
> Whose flocks supply him with attire,
> Whose trees in summer yield him shade,
> In winter, fire . . .

If *bread* once rhymed with *shade*, then it must have been pronounced as Devonians pronounce it today – braid. Again:

> . . . dreading e'en fools, by flatterers besieged,
> And so obliging, that he ne'er obliged . . .

Obliged must have been pronounced *obleeged*, as it still is in Devon. There must be many more examples. Dialectal pronunciation ought not to be dismissed as being a funny way of speaking conventional English. The dialectal pronunciation is frequently the original while the present-day standard English word has been derived from it. Dialect is thus frequently a repository of pronunciation and modes of speech once common but now archaic.

There are of course no rules, because dialect has never been and cannot be codified, and pronunciation has always varied from district to district, but some generalised observations can be made:

i.   The letter O is frequently pronounced as if it were an A. The word *stop* becomes *stap*, and the word *rot* turns into *rat*.
ii.   The double letter O appearing in the middle of a word often sounds like a U. *Stool* becomes *stule*, *fool* turns into *fule*

and *spoon* changes to *spune*.

iii.   Paradoxically, words containing the letter U often sound as if they are spelled with a double O. *Bull* becomes *bool*, and *pull* is *pool*. The same sound is heard in some words that have the letters OU or OW in them. *Bow* becomes *boo*, *mow* changes to *moo* and *plough* is *ploo*.

iv.   The sound best spelled ED (as in *head*) is frequently pronounced as if it were spelled AID. *Head* becomes *haid*, *dead* is *daid*, *leg* turns into *laig*, *Fred* into *Fraid* and so on, e.g. *'Fraid staied in baid wi' a bad laig, an now er's daid'*.

v.   The combined letters AR produce a sound like OR. Car becomes *cor*, *park* becomes *pork* and, of course a *car-park* is a *cor-park*. (It is interesting to note that this pronunciation survives in many parts of twentieth century USA). A *garden* is often a *gorden*, a *market* a *morket*, one does not play *darts*, but *dorts* and when it gets *dark* it is *dork*. *'Doan't ee work in the pork after dork!'*

vi.   The letter I frequently is pronounced as if it were a double E. *Hill* is *heel*, *will* is *weel*, *ill* is *eel*. *'Fraid lived up Torridge eel, but now er's daid and er left no weel'*.

vii.   Several words which end with the letters OL, EL, or LE (and therefore in standard English with the sounds EL or OL), are pronounced as if they ended with the letter O. *Mackerel* is *macrow* probably from the French *maquereau*, but *Bristol* becomes *Bristow* because the Old English name of the town was *Bryggstow*, meaning the place of the bridge, and has nothing to do with French. Another word is *trendle* which is pronounced *trendow* (a salting trough), although so far as I am aware, there is no French connection here either. Perhaps it is just easier to say O than it is to say OL or EL.

viii. There is always a tendency to place stress on word endings. Words which in standard English end with the letters ITE but are normally pronounced as if they ended with the letters IT are pronounced as they are spelled. *Favourite* is pronounced *fave-rite*, and *opposite* becomes *oppo-site*.

ix.   Initial letters are frequently pronounced in an unusual way.

Words beginning with the letters EN sound as if they begin with the letters IN. *Endeavour* becomes *indever* and *enterprising*, *interprising*.

x. *Every* becomes *ivery*.

xi. The initial letter F frequently becomes a V. *Field* becomes *vield*, *farmer* is *varmer* and *fen* becomes *venn*. (It is this transposition of initial letters which makes the tracking-down of dialect words so difficult. One can spend hours looking for a word which sounds as if it should begin with a V only to find it, hidden away in the dictionary, under F. The letter F is not the only example; there are many others.)

xii. Some say that all countrymen drop their aitches. This is not true. The letter H is not always aspirated, but it frequently is, quite positively and strongly.

xiii. I have seen it claimed somewhere that *zour* is a dialect word for *sour*. It is true that the initial S is often pronounced as if it were a Z, but this does not make it a dialect word.

xiv. The initial letters TH quite often sound as if they were DR. This is a very positive transformation and to many people *three* becomes *dree*, *throat* is *droat* or *drot* and *thrash* is *drash*.

xv. Other initial letters that are pronounced in an unorthodox way are UN and words like *uncomfortable*, *understand* and *unlikely* sound like *oncomfortable*, *onderstand* and *onlikely*.

xvi. There is often a tendency to split vowels and the word *dear* becomes *de-ar*, *fire* turns into *vi-yer* and *queer* is pronounced as *quee-yur*. Even a simple word like *here*, (usually pronounced *yur*) can become *hee-yar*.

xvii. Words like *really* and *lovely* are frequently pronounced as if they ended with AY. Thus *really* becomes *re-lay* and *lovely* sound like *love-lay*.

xviii. Letters within words are sometimes transposed, and this process, known as metathesis, turns a familiar standard word into what could be regarded as a dialect word since it is not simply subjected to change by pronunciation, but also by formation. *Crisp* becomes *crips*, *claps* replaces *clasp*, *lips* turn into *lisp*, *urch* is said instead of *rich* and *red* becomes *urd*.

There are very many examples including *wapses* or *wapsies* instead of the normal word *wasp*.

xix. The pronunciation of place names is of interest. Many villages and towns in Devon are of Saxon or pre-Saxon origin and have the suffix *worthy*. This is the modern spelling of the Saxon word *worthig*, meaning an enclosure, a yard about a house, an open place in a village or town or a homestead. Whatever the meaning, the suffix is usually pronounced URY or ERY or ARY, or REE. *Holsworthy* becomes *Holsery* or *Holsree*, *Bradworthy* is *Braddery* or *Bradree*, *Leeworthy* becomes *Leery* or *Leury*, *Exmansworthy* becomes *Engsree* and the long place names of *Alfardisworthy* and *Woolfardisworthy* are shortened to *Alsery* and *Woolsery*. In the latter case, the alternative WOOLSERY is frequently shown on signposts in brackets after the longer WOOLFARDISWORTHY.

VOCABULARY

Changes in Pronunciation of Standard English Words

THE list of words which follows is of recognisable changes by pronunciation of standard English words. There are, of course many more than I have listed. Some have been deliberately left out because they are of historical interest only and no longer in common use; others have been omitted for lack of space.

A

abn haven't

ace yes

aend end

affeared afraid

agin against

aich each

aid head

aigs eggs

aikel equal

ail eel

aimzes hames (part of a draught-horse's harness)

ait eat

aither either

aizy easy

all haul

aller alder (tree)

alse (see also **else**) else, otherwise

ango angle
ango-ire angle-iron
angshus anxious
anither another
ankcher handkerchief
ansum handsome
ant am not
apern apron
apmee halfpenny
apn happen
apse hasp (fastening on door) *'Doan't ferget ter apse the gate'*
arbs herbs
arby-pie a pie containing a lot of herbs: parsley, etc.
argify, argy to argue
arken listen, hearken
arrant errand
arter after
assards backwards (arse-wards)
ate eat
athout without, unless
attackted attacked
aud old
aughts and crosses noughts and crosses
aut (see also **awt** and **ort**) anything
auverdraw overthrow
aveered frightened
avire on fire
avore before, *'left avore'* – left handed

avore-aull after all, for all that
awiz always
awned owned, recognised
awp, awps hope *'Us ken awp ver zunshine'* – 'We can hope for some sunshine'
awt anything *'Do ee know awt bout this yer?'* – 'Do you know anything about this?'
awver over
ax to ask, to publish the banns of marriage
axed asked
ayend end
ay-er hair
ay-je hedge (see also chapter on etymology, the word *ay-je* is thought to come from the French *haie*)
ay-jey draw hedge trough, ditch, or drain along the bottom of a hedge
ay-jey-boar hedgehog
ay-uth, aith earth, soil, the world
ay-ve heave, throw
ayve-mun (aivmin) evening
azides besides
B
baal bawl, shout, talk roughly

backhouse, backouse back kitchen, wash house

backsivore backside, foremost, backwards

baid bed

bain been, bean

baint not going to, '*I baint*' – 'I won't'

bair beer

baistzez beasts (cattle, sheep)

baive beef

bam-bie by-and-by

bard bird

barriole barrel

beeve beef

bellerziz bellows, either for fire, blacksmith, or church organ

bellybon bellyband (part of a horse's harness, a girth)

bequath bequest

be-vower before

biddle beetle

bide stay (abide)

bigotive bigoted

bile boil

bile-in boiling

bimeby later (by-and-by)

bin been

bisky biscuit

bissle beastly, to make dirty

biy boy

bizzens business

blaid bleed

blaiged obliged

blid blood

bloo bloom

blooth bloom, blossom

boddle bottle

bool bull

booty beauty

borry to borrow

bost burst

bouta about

braid bread

brantitus bronchitis

bravey a job, a big job, a lot of work

braxis, braxus, brexis breakfast

brimbles, brimmles brambles

brish brush

britiful beautiful

brown titus bronchitis

bule bull

burches breeches

burge bridge

butchin butchering

bye boy

C

cafender carpenter

cannel candle

casn cannot

cat-ammed (cat-hammed) horses or cattle – or people – who have mis-shapen legs

caul kale, cabbage

caw-at coat

caze, cause occurence, case *'Tis usually the cause that dree frostzes be volleyed by rain'*

chack cheek (side of face)

channis challenge, argue with *'I didn't channis er!'*

cheel child (see also chapter on words and their meanings)

chewers chores, tasks

chid chit (allow something, usually potatoes, to sprout before planting)

chimber chamber, an upstairs room

chimley, chimbly chimney

chimley crook the hook in the chimney on which pots or kettles were hung

clat clod (of earth)

claws clothes

climmey climb

cliver clever, well (in health)

cloveray clover hay (hay made from temporary leys as opposed to hay made from permanent pastures)

clurk clerk

con-for-able comfortable

continny continue

coose coarse, rough in the sense of bad workmanship *'I doan't like ter zee concrete blocks mixed with stones in a dry-stonewall. Looks proper coose, you!'*

cornder corner

counton account

cracked correct *'It's cracked to come back'* – 'The correct thing to do is come back'

craim cream

crake creak

crake-along walk with difficulty

crap crop, *'crap o' teddies* – crop of potatoes

crilly-grains curly greens (type of kale)

crub a crumb, a crust (small piece of bread)

cuz because

D

Dabn, Debn, Dem, Demshur Devon (Devonshire)

daid dead

dairly dearly

dap tap (hit)
darter daughter
datchin thatching
deave deaf
dee die
deef deaf
deepth depth, something very subtle
dell deal (pinewood or inferior wood)
dezait deceit
dirteen thirteen
disnt-naw don't know
dister duster
dithn, dothn does not
doo two, too
doo-bail two-billed mattock
dood done *'Er dood it'*
dowel devil
drackly directly (usually means the very opposite: sooner or later)
draive drive
drash thresh
drasher a threshing machine
drauved drove (car, horse, etc.)
drawed throw
draw-up throw up (vomit), refer to the past in conversation
dray to draw, cart, carry, pull, take. *'Dray a pikchur'* – take a

photograph
dree three
drish thrush (bird)
drot throat
drowed throw, thrown
dug dog
dummun old woman
dunnaw don't know
durzant daren't (durst not)

E
easter eastern
ee, es yes
eel hill
een in
ees fay! Yes in faith! (an exclamation)
Else Alice (name)
empt empty *'It fair empted down!'* – 'It rained very hard!'
erbons ribbons
evelings evenings

F
feared afraid
feth, fey faith
frit frightened
furnt front
fuss theeng first thing (e.g. in the morning)

G
gain going
gaw! cor! (an exclamation)
ge-at gate
ge-at ook gate-hook,

fastening on gate
gee give
genst (hard g) against or
  towards
ginst, gin (hard g)
  against, towards
gonmer grandfather,
  grandmother
goosegog gooseberry
go'th goes (goeth)
graized greased
grammar grandmother
grampy grandfather
granfer grandfather
grin green
grovel gravel
gurrol girl
gurt great, large
guze goose
gwaine going

H
hab have
habn have not
hengous heinous, very
  large, terrible,
  tremendous
hey-go! hey-ho!
himperence impudence,
  impertinence

hinderment hindrance,
delay
holly holler (shout)
holt hold
hossifer officer
huffilant elephant

I
iggerant ignorant
ijit idiot
infermation inflammation
injin engine
innards inwards (as in
  'inward parts')
intertainment
  entertainment
iss* yes
izzel himself

J
jean gin
jidge judge
jolk jolt
jumbo-zale jumble sale

K
kay key, quay
ketch catch
kit kite, any hawk or bird
  of prey
knacked knocked
koncekense consequence

---

*This is a less of a word than an indrawn breath between the
teeth and over the tongue. It signifies 'yes', general agreement,
and indication of sympathy, or merely an invitation to the person
to whom one is listening to carry on with his tale.

krackt correct
kwai-it quiet

L

laanch launch
lade laden, load
laf lath (as in lath and
  plaster)
laffed laughed
laig leg
lain lean
laive leave
larn learn
law a load
leaf leave (as in furlough)
leel little
leet little
lem eleven
lent loaned
lew loo, lee (sheltered,
  from the wind)
lewness being sheltered
  from the wind
lewth a shelter or
  something that gives
  protection from the
  wind
lewzide sheltered side (of
  hedge or building)
lookee! see! (look ye!)
losting losing
louster litter, waste by
  littering, also work hard
  *'Them as can't scheemy
  must louster'* – if one is
  not brainy (not able to
  'scheme') one must

work with one's hands
luvver lover (usually term
  of endearment as
  opposed to the more
  usual meaning)

M

maddick mattock
maister master, boss
margit market
marvels marbles
mashes marshes
masony masonry,
  working as a mason
ma-ur moor, wet ground
mauth, mose moss
mazed, maized amazed,
  daft
me-art might
meel meddle, interfere
  with
meeze mice
min, mun man, 'them'
mokus monkey
morket market
moulder mould
mulkee to milk
mushelroom mushroom
mux muck
muxy mucky, muddy or
  dirty

N

nacken een! knock it
  (nail, gate post, etc) in!
  'Nacken een the aid!'
  (literally, knock it in the
  head) 'Stop doing

whatever you are doing;
give up!'
nair near, mean,
tight-fisted
nawed knew
nawse nose
nawtiz notice
neeze sneeze
niver never
noan none
nointed wicked (anointed,
used in the sense of the
devil's anointed)
nort naught, nothing
norther northern
nother neither, another
nuff enough
O
ockered awkward
Offy Alfie, Alfred (name)
omm oven
oncomferable
uncomfortable
ondaicent indecent,
uncivil
ondaicentness indecency
one-tother one-another
onlight alight (from a car,
horse, etc.)
on-nawin unknowing
onpossible impossible
onproper improper
onthaw to thaw (some
thing)
onwriggler irregular,
uneven, unpunctual

ood wood
ook hook
oo-mun woman
ope open
ormers alms
ort aught, nothing, ought
orted hurt, injured
orwiz always
owdacious audacious
owzum-iver however
P
paice peace, piece
palled turned pale
paltrige partridge
pankin panting
passel parcel, quantity,
package, collection
passen parson
pauss post
pawer poor, pour, to
cram or to stuff full
peel pillow
peel-bears pillowcases
peg pig
pernt print
pimrose primrose
pisky, piskie, pixie
pisky laid caused by the
pixies to lose one's
direction
pitchin pitching, throwing
pittis pity
planchin planking,
floorboards
plat plot of land
polyanties polyanthus

pool pole, poll, top of head

popple, popplestone pebble, pebblestone

posses, postses posts (usually gate-posts)

powsen poison *'When us fust got main watter, twas just like powsen! Us cuddn't make a propper cuppa tay'*

prang prong, hayfork

prapper proper, good, satisfactory

primrosen primrose

pun upon

purtickly particularly

purvekshun perfection

Q

queear queer

quelstring sweltering, very hot (weather)

quot, quat squat, stoop (used about any animal which flattens itself on the ground to escape observation)

R

radded rotted

raich reach

rail revel, jollification

rames remains, remnants, skeleton

rare raw (underdone)

rasselin wrestling

ratted rotted

raud row, road

raw row

re-diklus ridiculous

rid red

rile royal

rin run

risty rusty

rittle rattle (in the throat)

rittling heavy or hard breathing

rouser, rouster someone making a great noise

rout rut, wheel track

rowcast rough-cast

rummage rubbish

S

sassy saucy, lively, spirited

sauger soldier

saw soul *'I'm veared to me saw'* – 'I'm frightened to my soul' (frightened to death)

scabby shabby (dirty trick)

scat scatter or throw, go *scat* – to become bankrupt (see *squat*)

scollard scholar

scritch shriek

scruff scurf or dandruff

sex sect (church or chapel)

shape sheep

shaw show (as in County Show)

shet shut, shoot

shillett shale, sedimentary rock

shitten, shitty paltry, mean, base, contemptible, dirty

shoole shovel

shore-nuff sure enough, certainly, no doubt

showel, shoel shovel

shreed shred

sife, sify sigh

siggle giggle, snigger, titter

sinney sinew

sive scythe

sivver several, a good many

skeen skin

skimmish squeamish

skivver skewer (made of wood)

slomes, slones sloe (the fruit of the blackthorn)

smarless smallest

solger soldier

souther southern

spaik speak of, talk about

speckerty speckled (usually applied to poultry e.g. '*a speckerty hen*')

spuddle to struggle, kick, resist capture, to be busy in a useless way

spuddlin struggling, poking about

spurticles spectacles

squat to squash, crush, squeeze, '*go squat*' to become bankrupt (see *scat*)

staint to staunch '*staintin blid*' – to staunch a flow of blood

standing a standing place in a market or a stall for horses or cattle

stanks stinks

stann! stand still! (to horse)

stapped stepped

starded started

stauld stolen

stauve stove

steep to stoop, lay a hedge

stenks stinks, smells

stent stunt, to cause to cease to grow

sterrage a 'stir up' (fuss or commotion)

steve to stiffen, to be stiff, to be numb, to freeze (mostly used of frost or cold)

stiffel stifle

stoopid stupid

stram slam, to bang

stub stump (of a bush or piece of wood)

stugged stuck (in the mud or snow)

stummick stomach or appetite *'A gude stummick to ee wun an all'*

sudger, sodger soldier

T

tar tear, break, be in a passion or rage

tarnal eternal

taw'd toad, a person, *'poor ol' taw'd', 'silly ol' taw'd'*

tay tea (usually the meal)

tayjess tedious

teddy, tiddy potato

tegeddle tea-kettle

tegeddle-brauth, tiggitle-brauth tea-kettle broth (bread soaked in milk and served with butter, salt and pepper)

tiddivate titivate

tiddn tis not, it isn't

titch-en-tight touch and go

toze tease, as in disentangling, to comb or card wool

trade tread

traw, trow trough

turmits turnips

turrible terrible

twadden it was not

twick tweak (to jerk suddenly)

U

ugs puddin hogs pudding (a local kind of pork sausage)

ulse else

ungered hungry

up auver up above (up over)

upzot upset

urch rich

urd red

uthout without, unless, except

V

vahl fall, a fall of rain or snow

vaityers features (looks)

vall autumn

vall back, vall edge come what may (heads or tails)

valley value

var far

varder farther

vardist farthest

varmer* farmer

varmering farming

varmint vermin

---

* Still used as a title. One will greet a person 'Good morning, Farmer', or ask 'Do you know Farmer Wonnacott?'

vast fast, eager

vatches vetches (*leguminosae*)

vaur before, in front of, until, for

vaur day before day – before daylight

vaurn for him (for 'un)

vaur-parrut the forward part, front

vaur-um 'Get in front', 'Get before them' – a shepherd's order to his dog to get in front of his sheep

vayacles vehicles

veared afraid (feared)

veesh fish

vencrake fen-crake, landrail, corncrake

venn fen

ver far

verder further

verdist furthest

vetch fetch

vethervaw feverfew (plant)

vetinry veterinary surgeon

viredug fire-dog, andiron

vittles victuals (food)

vitty fitting, suitable, correct

vittyness fittingness, dexterity, neat-handedness

vloor floor

vlower flower

voaks folks, people, work people

volley to follow

voot foot

vor before, in front of

vore on, forward, going forth, four

vorenoon morning (forenoon)

voretoken forewarning

vot fault

votees photographs

vrim from

vry fool

vur, vaur for

vurriner foreigner, any stranger (even someone from the next village)

vur-why 'For why?' – 'Why, because' (in a statement)

vuzz furze, gorse

W

waarn warrant

wad whet (a scythe or knife)

waj wedge, bet or wager

walvin wallowing, rolling in dust as do fowls and animals

ware, wur, weather

way with

way-in within

way'n with him

wellzaid 'Well said' (an

indication of approval)

werry weary

wester western

whiles while, whilst

whippintree whipple tree (draught bar for horses)

why'n ee why don't you

wick weak

wive wife

Wi-yum William

wopsey wasp

worts, urts whortleberries

wude would

wurd hoard

wurdle world

wuth worth

wuts oats

Y

yaffer heifer

yap to bark (yap) like a terrier

yappin yapping (talking a lot)

yarbs herbs

yaw ewe, yew tree

yaw cat female cat

yer an ear, here, to hear, come here

yerd tell heard (heard tell)

yerzel yourself

yet heat

yeth heath, heather

yettin heating

yurrin a hearing, trial

Z

zackly exactly

zad the letter Z

zaive sieve

zalt salt

zand sand

zap sap (in wood or vegetables)

zartain certain

zauney simple, (daft)

zebun seven

zeed-out to seed out, sow land with grass seeds

zel self

zex, zax zax (a chopping tool used by slaters)

zex sect, denomination (Church of England, Methodist, etc.)

zhure sure, certain

zie, zieth a scythe

zill sell *'nort fer zill'* – nothing to sell

zim to seem *'I zim'* – 'it seems to me'

zin sun

zinney sinew

zixteen sixteen

zlatter scatter

znaw snow

zoonder sooner (rather)

zore sore

zot sat

zummat something

zupper supper

zwar, zwaur swathe

zye scythe

3

GRAMMAR

GRAMMAR is defined by the OED as 'That department of the study of a language which deals with rules . . . the system of inflections and syntactical usages . . .'

Eric Partridge, in his *Usage and Abusage*, warned students to beware of falling into the error of supposing that there was such a thing as a universal grammar which was applicable to every language. He stressed that grammar has no existence apart from language. It is, in short, a set of rules codifying usage and it does not pre-determine usage. Grammar is made for man, not man for grammar.

It is certainly clear that what was at one time held to be grammatically acceptable may readily become unacceptable, and *vice versa*. The grammar of dialect must not be dismissed as being wrong simply because it departs from or does not conform to rules which now govern standard English usage.

In 1877 Elworthy published a paper on the grammar of West Somerset, and Pearse Chope, in his paper on the dialect of Hartland, agreed that it was not unlike the grammar of the North Devon dialect. Sarah Hewett went to some lengths to comment on grammatical construction in 1892, but all three were perhaps attempting to codify a language form which cannot be codified without hastening its disappearance. Indeed, it was the declared purpose of the academics of the seventeenth and eighteenth centuries to superimpose grammatical rules upon the rude speech of their times and so to produce a standard language.

Despite this, there are certain patterns of speech and usage which are of interest, so long as it is recognised that they are NOT rules, and never have been. If they were to be made into rules, this would further help destroy that which many seek to preserve.

PLURAL ENDINGS

ELWORTHY claimed that there were eight forms of plural terminations in West Somerset dialect nouns. I suspect that three of these are now obsolete, but five certainly still exist, and whilst there are countless examples, I list below one of each, showing first the standard English word in its singular form, then the dialect version in the singular and in the plural.

1. rheumatic	*roomatik*	*roomatiks*	(ending *s*)
2. fool	*vool*	*voolz*	(ending *z*)
3. frost	*vrost*	*vrostez*	(ending *ez*)
4. child	*cheel*	*chiller*	(ending *r*)
5. wasp	*wapse*	*wapzies*	(ending *zies*)

SIMILES

ELWORTHY and Sarah Hewett gave a lot of space to similes and there are enough of these to fill a book. I will list just a few.

Many refer to degrees of stupidity: *daft as a handcart, mazed as a brish, queer as Dick's hatband.* (Nineteenth century: 'as queer as Dick's hatband, that went nine times round and would not meet').

A lot of similes refer to degrees of anger or fierceness: *wild as an 'awk, wild as a badger, mad as a Scot, mad as an Irish.*

Others of interest are *straight as a gun barrel, whist as a winnard* – meaning as miserable as a heron. (I like this one because nothing looks quite so miserable as a grey heron standing by a stream). Something or someone can be *zour as a grab* (crab-apple), and one frequently hears the slightly indelicate but graphic expression, *as tight as a fish's (or duck's) arse.* This is used to describe either a degree of physical tightness, or someone who is tight-fisted. One can be as *poor as a coot*, and in the end a person or a thing can be *daid as a stump.*

Other graphic similes range from the self-explanatory observation *'Er's as plain as an ol' gate'* to the criticism *'You'm like a hen avore day'* ('You are completely disorganised'). One will say of something unripe *'T'is so green as a lik'* 'lik = leek the vegetable,' and of a silly child or even a silly adult, *'Er's so daft as a raddow'* (raddow = rattle although it is not clear why a rattle should be daft). An impatient fellow workman might say of another standing about in an awkward useless fashion *'You'm like a goose wi' the sprawls'*. (Geese sometimes suffer with an ailment locally called 'the sprawls' which makes it difficult for them to stand up), or the same workman might say of a mate who complained of the tough nature of the job in hand, *'You'm so saft as a teddy,'* (teddy = potato).

EE AND ER

IN Devon, as in other counties where tourists visit, dialect is not always treated sensibly either by the locals, who ought to know better, or by new-comers who also ought to respect the language of their adopted county, or by visitors who simply come to enjoy themselves. There are many examples of cashing-in on dialect and making fun of it. Souvenirs of all kinds, postcards, china mugs probably made in Hong Kong, and calendars are inscribed with 'local' sayings designed to bring a smile to the face of the uncomprehending foreigner. The apparent misuse of the masculine and feminine third person singular pronoun gives rise to much amusement. One of the popular sayings to which I refer is *'In Debn, ee's an er, an er's an ee, all 'ceptin' my Missus' ol' tom cat, an' even ee's an er!'*

The use of the word which sounds like *er* or *ur*, is not necessarily a bucolic idiosyncracy, although in some contexts it is an unaspirated *her*. The OED records that the word *her* is a close relative to the Dutch *Heer* and the German *Herr*, both of which are masculine. The word was originally used as a form of address to superiors and is connected with the word *hoary* ('hoary with age', meaning venerable). A *here-man* was a Lord or Master, and the OED gives many examples of the use of the masculine word *here* during the ninth to fourteenth centuries. It says that the word is 'used by Welsh or Gaelic speakers for he, him or for the speaker himself . . .' and Halliwell (*c.*1847) records that in the West of England *er* meant *he*. It still does, at least at times.

Whether or not the sound *er* is an aspirated *her* or a word in its own right, the masculine *er* is undoubtedly used, but so is the masculine *he* and *him* and *his*. These are also frequently used for obviously feminine things. One will hear it said of a cow, for example, *'he's* off his food but *he's* suckling *ee's* calf'.

The second person singular is still quite often *thee,* and this is abbreviated to *ee*. *Thee* (thou) *art* becomes *thee-rt* or even *thee't*. The words *thou* and *ye* are in daily use but the word that sounds like *ee* can be just an unaspirated *he*. It may, however, be an abbreviated *ye* or *thee*. 'Do'st *ee*?' means doest thee?

BIST

THE Anglo-Saxon word *bist* is in regular use. It means what it has always meant: *art* or *thou art*. Chope gave two examples in 1881: 'Thee *bist* the biggest vule I ever did zee!' and *'Bist* gwain vor to do aught today?' These are as alive today as they were a hundred years ago.

US

THE word *us* is used rather curiously, but regularly, as a nominative: *'Us* be gwain ter morket' or *'Us* be sot be the vire'.

TH

IN the present tense, the ending *th* is used in the third person singular and the first and second persons plural: *It goeth, it rinneth* (runs), *us calleth, they telleth, yer liveth, er putteth,* and as an old lady once said to me about the weather, 'Us must take what *cometh!'*

LIKE

ONE frequently hears expressions such as 'Er sings *loud-like'* (meaning that someone sings loudly), or 'Doctor comed *quick-like',* which is self-explanatory.

The suffix *like* is probably what remains of the middle English *lich* which has become the standard English suffix *ly.* Thus, what sounds like *loud-like* and *quick-like* might more properly be spelled *loud-lich* and *quick-lich. Angered-like* means very angry and 'Er can't hear *much-like'* means that he is very deaf.

THAT, WHAT FOR

THE word *so,* when used to describe a degree of something (so cold, so angry), is often replaced in dialect by the word *that.* 'I were *that* cold' or 'Us wus *that* angered'. The simple question *why?* is often replaced by *what for? 'What vor* did 'ee do that?'

ELSE

THE dialectal use of the adverb *else* is particularly interesting and serves to indicate the antiquity of the dialectal language form. In modern English the adverb invariably follows an indefinite pronoun meaning either *in addition* or *instead,*

('Anything else?' or 'What else?'). This was not always so. In its original use the word had a force of its own and was an adjective used absolutely. It is still so used in dialectal speech. 'Hurry up cheel, us'll be late *else!*', 'Betterway mend that roof, it'll leak *else!*' The OED gives several examples of this original usage and I have found several in Shakespeare. The best, because of its direct relationship with present day Devon dialect, is in King Henry VIII in which the Lord Chamberlain says 'Come, good Sir, we shall be late *else!*'

TO

THE preposition *at* is often replaced by the word *to*. The examples are self-explanatory. 'Where's e *to?*', 'Last Tuesday us was *to* Bideford', 'Us'll do un *to* dinnertime'. It is interesting to note that in many cases the word *to* is replaced by the word *for*. In archaic standard English the two words were frequently used together, e.g. 'She went to market, her eggs *for to* sell', 'But what went ye out *for to* see?', 'Simple Simon went a fishing, *for to* catch a whale'.

In Devon dialect, the word *to* has disappeared leaving only the word *for* (*fer*). The above quotations would become 'Er went *fer* market, er eggs *fer* zill', 'But what went 'ee out *fer* zee?', '. . .a fishing *fer* catch a whale'.

More common phrases that are used every day: 'I want *fer* knaw' ('I want to know'), 'I've got nort *fer* zill' ('I've nothing to sell'), 'Us went *fer* Bideford' ('We went to Bideford').

The word *to* is also used in the sense of belonging to. 'There baint no key *to* this door', 'Be there a garden *to* this cottage?'

YOU

MANY statements end with the word *you*! This merely adds emphasis. 'My, tiz cold, *you!*' implies that it is really *very* cold indeed. There are many examples in which the word *you* becomes a kind of verbal exclamation mark. 'Speaks of rain, *you*', or 'Wot be bout, *you*?'

SINGULAR AND ADJECTIVAL ENDINGS

IT is of more than passing interest to note that, while the plural form of an ancient word is retained in standard English, sometimes the singular occurs only in dialect. Perhaps the best example is the word *brethren* which, though archaic, is still used particularly in place names, such as 'Seven Brethren'. The singular, *brether* is the dialect word for *brother*. In rather the same way some adjectives that are no longer in common use describe nouns which are still with us. *Glassen* is the dialect word for something made of glass, and *cloamen* is something made of cloam (clay). There is no rule and the process is reversed in the modern adjective *iron* which describes the dialect noun *ire*, which means iron. (See *bar ire*, and *ango ire*).

THE grammar of dialect is often mixed with ungrammatical present day English. It is easy to confuse the two and difficult to decide where one ends and the other starts. It could even be that what we now regard as ungrammatical English is, at least in part, a survival of dialectal usage.

4

WORDS AND THEIR USAGE

IT is probably the unusual use of standard English words, flavoured with local accent and pronunciation, which most bewilders or amuses visitors to the county.

Ordinary words acquire new meanings. People, places and meal-times have unfamiliar names, and seemingly meaningless 'noises' are often heard in fields and in farmsteads. In this section I will list a few examples.

NAMES FOR PEOPLE

AN interesting practice survives in Devon, somewhat similar to that which exists in Wales and perhaps elsewhere, whereby it is not unusual for a person to give him or herself an identifying suffix. There are so many people with the same surnames that additional identification is often necessary. It makes a lot of sense, for example, for a Mr Heard to indicate which one he is out of the one hundred and fifty or more people of the same surname who appear in the North and West Devon and North East Cornwall telephone directory. So a farmer will announce himself on the telephone as *Heard to Southcott or John to Southcott*, making positive identification possible. Another may call himself *Eric Binnery* indicating that his Christian name is *Eric* and he farms at Binworthy, or a woman may identify herself as *Dorothy Waytown* meaning that her name is Dorothy and that she lives at Waytown. There is also a tendency to name people by their occupations, and *Fred-down-garrige, Elsie-up-shop* and *Alfie-over-pub* are by no means unusual.

FIELD NAMES

FIELD names, like place names, are a special study. Many are of great antiquity but others are still being awarded. Not two miles from my home there are two fields, one called *In-front-of George's* and the other *Behind-Jack's*. Neither George nor Jack live there any more, but the field will bear their names until they are buried under the concrete and tarmac of progress, probably long after people have forgotten who George and Jack were.

MEALS

A visitor to Devon can easily be confused by the names given to meals. 'Lunch' is a substantial meal eaten at about ten o'clock and consisting of what most people would normally eat for breakfast. It is sometimes called breakfast or *braxis*, but it is more normally 'lunch'.

What many people in other parts of the country call 'lunch' is known as 'dinner'. Dinner in the evening is usually reserved for meals eaten in an hotel or for annual functions of Associations and Societies. The usual evening meal is called tea or *tay* and this is eaten at about six o'clock after the evening milking is finished. This is a substantial meal consisting of meat and vegetables followed by cakes, cut-rounds, jam and cream. One will hear a wife say 'Us must get on 'ome and cook *tay*'.

To the uninformed perhaps this sounds a little odd, but she means only that she must get home in time to prepare the evening meal.

NOISES

THESE are not words, but they are frequently heard and deserve a place in this book.

Ho! ho! ho! (sometimes almost ko! ko! ko! with the 'k' implosive)	Noise made when calling cows to come for milking.
Peg! peg! peg!	Call for pigs
Loo! loo! loo!	Noise made to frighten birds or rabbits from corn or grass which is about to be cut

THE MISUSE OF WORDS

CERTAIN standard English words are regularly misused for no apparent reason. Whether this was once a deliberate attempt to be amusing and has become habitual, or whether there has always been a genuine misunderstanding is impossible to say. Whatever the reason, certain words are regularly misused and, as such, have become a part of the dialect of the county.

It is important to treat such misuses with caution, because some have been created by writers attempting to give an impression of dialect. A. J. Coles who wrote under the pen name of *Jan Stewer* said in the preface to his book *Ole Bisket* that he had not written his book with an eye to the etymologist, but for the amusement of his readers. Those who have read Jan Stewer's books will know that some of his dialect words appear to be his own invention. He calls a car accelerator an *acsillyrater* and says that it is a good name for it because it 'acts silly'. He calls the carburettor the *carbreaker,* and while he may have heard someone use these words, they should not be accepted without question as being true dialect in general use. Indeed, this is borne out by Jan Stewer himself who in the glossary of one of his books says of the word *cherrybim* (cherubim) that he had 'actually heard an old man so describe a charabanc'.

Nevertheless, the accidental or deliberate misuse of foreign words is the very stuff of which the English language is made. Consider for example, the etymology of the word clove. This word comes from the French words *clou de girofle* which means literally 'nail of *girofle* (the flower)', and it refers to the appearance of the seed which looks very much like a nail of the kind that used to be manufactured by the village blacksmith. Either through a misunderstanding, or more likely because of the inability of the English to pronounce the words correctly, the phrase became shortened and the only word used was *clou*. This in turn evolved into 'clove', so the English cook who puts a clove into a rice pudding or a baked apple is putting a French nail into it. The story does not end there. The second part of the French phrase (*girofle*) still survives but has turned into the word *gillyflower*, the countryman's name for either a wallflower or a species of pink that is known to many as a clove pink, because it smells like a clove.

It is no more, or less, amusing to speak of putting a French nail into a pudding than to use some of the phrases that follow.

'*Arrest* assured I be all right!'

'Er's lookin' up 'er *auntcestors*' (ancestors)

'Er's a bit *bigotive* like!' (bigoted)

'That roof be leakin' like a *calendar*'

'Our Emily is bein' *created* over Barnstaple crematorium'

'Where be they *destructions* for this yer tractor?' (instruction manual)

'They say us've gotter 'ave one of they ole *distinguishers*' (fire extinguishers)

'Be I *illegible* for a grant?'

'If our speaker doant turn up zoon, us'll have ter *impoverish* summat' (improvise)

'Be you *intimidating* that I doant knaw wot I be tellin' about?' (intimating)

'I be aveared of they dirty Atom bombs! One of these day us'll get 'urtled into *maternity*!'

'Our Bert 'ad to see one of they ole *physical therapists*' (physio.)

'I woant 'ave they childer *protruding*' (intruding)

'If us goes in they woods, us'll get *persecuted*' (prosecuted)

'The Torridge District Council've put out *refuge* collection to contract'

MEDICAL AND HEALTH

Devonians are probably no more or less concerned with their health than other people else but they sometimes seem to have difficulty with medical terms. Perhaps this is a defence mechanism that deliberately makes fun of serious matters or maybe it is yet another manifestation of the deliberate or accidental misuse of words.

Arthur-itis	arthritis
Brown-titus	bronchitis
Limp glands	(lymph)
Occupational	terrorists
Physical	therapists
Prostrate	trouble

VOCABULARY

Change in Use of English Words and Phrases

SOME of the words and phrases that follow reflect the Devonian's sense of humour, others have become clichés, and as such, form part of our dialect.

In order to present them in reasonable order I have selected the principal word in each phrase or sentence and used this to determine its alphabetical place in the list.

A

take un abroad take it to pieces

'I'm always achin an crakin' aching and creaking (in the joints)

next akin close to, almost
'*Er weren't daid, but next akin to it*'

all *so well* just as well

'I **allow** *that the lifeboat
got too near they rocks'*
'I believe that...' (this is
an example of a word
no longer in general use
in England but which
survives in dialect and is
used in present-day
American speech)

back **along** a while ago,
some time ago, years
ago

'There's no **anger** *in't'*
(Referring to the cloud
on the horizon and
meaning that it is not
likely to rain)

wild as an **'awk** (hawk)
very angry, very fierce
(animal or human)

B

go **back,** *going* **back** to
deteriorate. *'Er's goin
back vast'* – he, or it, is
deteriorating rapidly

back *ouse* (house) back
kitchen, scullery,
lean-to, wash house

bacon-*aid* (head) dunce,
stupid person

wild as a **badger** angry

a **belly** *like a Barnstaple
man, a* **bum** *like a
Barnstaple woman.* Pot
bellied, anyone, male or
female, with a big

backside. It may be
merely because the letter
B looks vaguely like a
bulging human figure
but it has been
suggested to me that the
expressions, quite
frequently heard, relate
to the relative prosperity
of Barnstaple in the
past, which could
perhaps have caused its
citizens to grow fat. I
consider that it is more
likely to be derogatory
in intent and related to
the long-standing
differences between
Bideford and Barnstaple,
whose citizens still
argue and even fight
over the number of
ships each port sent to
fight the Spanish
Armada in 1588.

'Where was you to **beer,
Sunday?'** 'Which pub
did you patronise last
Sunday?'

before superior to, better
than *'Ridin is before
walkin'*

better *way* one had
better, it is better that
one should (another
example of a phrase

which is lost in standard English but survives in modern American usage.)

bettermost *volk* probably best described as upper-middle-class people

between *the two lights* twilight (the two lights being the sun and the moon)

my **bird** a form of affectionate address between people, male to female, female to female or even male to male

blackaid (black-head) tadpole

black *drish* (thrush) blackbird

black *tail* a stoat

me **booty** My beauty. A form of address to men, women and animals quite indiscriminately, irrespective of the sex of the speaker or of the person or animal being addressed

bow bend '*See if you can bow un straight*'. This is interesting usage because in standard English the word bow tends to imply the bending into a curve something that was once straight. In Devon it means to bend into a curve *or* to straighten something that is bent.

boy *chap* an unimportant or unimpressive young man

brave an amplifying word '*a brave lot*' – a lot, '*a brave ol uproar*' – an unpleasant state of confusion or noise. The word also means 'well' or 'fine': '*Ow be gettin on then*?' – 'How do you do?' elicits the answer: '*Brave, oh brave*!'

break to tear. One *breaks* a piece of cloth

bullocks any bovine animal, including dairy cattle. Dairy cows are 'milking bullocks'

C

canvas linoleum, floor covering including modern equivalent of linoleum

caper any activity or happening. A general election might be called '*thees ol 'lection caper.*' There is often a

suggestion of dis-
approval of the subject
under discussion.

***Doan't take no nawtis
zur, the* change *o' life
went to her aid*** (head)
Husband explaining
irrational behaviour of
his wife

cheel (child) a baby girl.
Parents of a new-born
baby will be asked '*Be
it a biye or a cheel?*'
(See Shakespeare's *The
Winter's Tale*' Act III,
Scene III. Shepherd:
'What have we here?
[Taking up the child]
Mercy on's, a bairn; a
very pretty bairn! A boy
or a child, I wonder?)
The word *cheel* is also
used as a term of
endearment by a
husband and wife:
'*Come along cheel, us'd
better-way get whoam*'

chilled slightly warmed,
(the chill taken off)
'*Us've chilled the water*'

**'*plenty of* cider *in that
there chimbley*'** said of
a badly built chimney
stack

clever in good health.
Normally used in a

negative sense; '*Er baint
too clever, you*!' This
means that the person
concerned is very
unwell

coller *en aimzes* collar
and tie. The collar and
hames are part of a
working horse's harness
and go around the
animal's neck; '*Us puts
on coller en aimzes fer
go ter chapel*'

coller work very hard
work. The expression
dates from the time
when a working horse
pulling a heavy load
pressed hard into its
collar

'*Er's* corkin' *an' gwain*'
He is carrying on
despite an irritating
cough left over from a
heavy cold

couple a ewe with lambs.
A 'single couple' is a
ewe with one lamb, a
'double couple' is one
with twin lambs and a
sheep with triplets is a
'triple couple'

***passel of ol* crams**
something not worthy of
credence

crist crust '*My ol' tractor*

*wouldn't pull the crist off
a rizepudden!'*
criterion consideration,
importance. Usually
used negatively: *'That
baint no criterion'*
cross *way* a road junction.
A *four cross-way* is a
normal cross road. A
three cross-way is a T
or Y junction
D
It **dabs** *in early these days*
Nights are drawing in
'Ave'ye yurd 'bout Emily?'
– *'Naw. Er's* **daid***!' –
'Ree-lay! I didn't knaw
as er was sick, what was
the trouble?' – 'Oh,
nothing see-rious you!'*
   *'Us haven't seen ol'
Jan for some time. Er
waddn't to Chapel
anniversay last wik.
Naw, er's daid, er'd a
come else!'*
   A man was found
hanging in a barn:
*'Why didn't ye cut er
down? – 'I didn't knaw
if er was daid!'*
my **dear** not usually a
term of affection
although it is, of course,
used in the normal
context. It is more likely
to be used as a form of
address to anyone, not
necessarily someone
known familiarly
demand command *'Stay
there an' you'll be able
to demand both ways'*,
said to sentry or watch-
man or any person ap-
pointed to be a look-out
for any purpose.
dirty a word of amplification normally
implying something
tiresome or troublesome.
A dirty shame – a
terrible shame, *a dirty
foreigner* – someone
from a long way off (as
opposed to an ordinary
foreigner who could be
just someone from the
next parish). *'I've not
done a dirty thing in my
garden'* – I've achieved
little in the garden. (The
word dirty is only used
to mean unclean when
standard English is
being mixed with
dialect. The dialect word
for dirty is *bissle*.)
distinct distinguish, see
clearly, recognise. *'I
couldn't distinct un
proper'*

dough *baked* half baked, silly, soft in the head

Er **drashed** *un wi watter* drenched

dry-*belly* a miser

E

goodnight **each** *goodnight everybody*

F

proper **fashion** When used to amplify a statement, it means 'well and truly' *'Us be znawed-een* [snowed-in] *proper fashion*

put fast fasten, close, shut (door or gate)

fetch *the pump* prime the pump to produce sufficient suction to allow it to raise water

firelights kindling for lighting fires (as opposed to *sticks* which are logs)

my **flower** another normal form of address between friends of either sex. I have heard this used as a form of address between two robust and very masculine farmers

forestry a plantation managed by the Forestry Commission *'Our Trevor works up forestry'*. One also goes for a walk *'in the forestry'*.

frightened surprised *'I were frightened to zee zo many volk up Church'*

G

gentry *volk* gentry, upper-class people

serve ee **glad** it serves you right

'That there tractor of your'n couldn't pull **Granny** *off the pot!'*

that do make the **gravy** *run* hard work that makes one sweat

bout a **gunshot** a measure of distance (said to be approximately the distance between two telegraph poles)

H

only **half** *a load* simple, not quite right in the head

play **Hamlet** kick up a fuss, create a scene. *'Er didn't alf play Amlet!'*

daft as a **handcart** stupid, silly

handsome beautiful, worthy of praise, good *'A handsome morning'*, or *'Ow be then my*

flower?' – 'Andsome
me dear, proper
andsome'

me **handsome** yet another
normal form of address,
friendly but not
necessarily familiar

'Us'll zee wot the weather
happens' 'We will see
what happens to the
weather'

a proper **harem-scarum**
a rascal, a wild
uncontrolled person

queer as Dick's **hatband**
strange, unusual, odd
person

up th' **eel** (hill) on higher
ground, particularly on
the moors. *'Er varms up
th' eel'* probably means
that he farms on
Exmoor or Dartmoor

a **hinderment** a delay *'Us
met wi a hinderment'*

'Us can't call him **home'**
'We cannot remember
him'

'The watter was up **home**
to the tap o'me butes'
'The water came up to
the top of my boots'

hundreds a lot, plenty,
many *'Come on een,
there's undreds of
room', or 'Us've got*

hundreds of grass you!'
(Until 1469, the word
hundred merely
meant more than five
score)

I

ignorant (iggerant) bad
mannered, badly
brought up, foolish or
uncouth behaviour.
*'Doan't ee take no
notice of Bill Brewer,
er's propper iggerant',*
(said of a rude,
outspoken person)

J

job a happening, an event
(see *caper*) *'Thees ol'
lection job'*

K

kidneybain runner bean

L

learn (larn) teach

litany *of complaints* long
list of complaints

long-sleeve *clock*
grandfather clock

long-sleeve *hat* top hat

long-tailed *rabbut*
pheasant (sometimes
shot without a game
licence, when it is
'mistaken' for a rabbit)

M

made meanings to make
facial signs or gestures

maid little girl, young woman not necessarily a virgin, a term of enderment used by a man addressing his wife no matter how old she might be

manful powerful *'Baint manful enough you!'*

manys-a-time often

marvellous something at which to marvel. In modern speech the word usually means something good, but this is not so in dialect. *'Tiz marvellous ter zee zuch bad ploughin'*

master another amplifying word; *master big* – very big, *master small* – very small, *master cold* – very cold. (The word is pronounced much as in standard English, but mister (Mr), a word derived from master, is pronounced *maister,* retaining the old French pronunciation *maistre*)

mazed *as a brish* daft, stupid, (a *brish* is a brush, although why a brush should be stupid is not clear)

by his **mind** of his own free-will *'Er wouldn't go up Doctor's by ee's mind, but us made un'*

no **mistake** still another amplifying phrase *'Us be znawed een,* [snowed in] *no mistake!'*

mortal, mort a considerable quantity, very. Used to amplify: *'There's a mortal lot ov it about', 'I'm a mortal onlucky ol chap', 'There was a mort of volk up Church'*

N

near mean, tight-fisted

neither *'Us saw a chap to Barnstaple t'other day. Er looked at I, an' I looked at er, an' we thought us rekernised one t'other, so us crossed the road an' when us got to the middle, t'waddn't neither on us!'*

about **nort** doing nothing, idle *'Av' ee got a lorry about nort?* 'Have you got a spare lorry?'

zhure **nuff** (enough) yet another phrase of amplification: *'Us be znawed een, zhure nuff!'*

O

ordained ruled, agreed, decided *'Twas ordained fur me to do the job'*

don't make a bit ov **odds** I don't mind if I do

P

parish *lantern* the moon

passel *of rummage* (rubbish) a parcel of rubbish, nonsense

'They'm pickin' from our **pen** *now, Chap'* said to a contemporary when a friend died. (At a market or abattoir beasts are penned in groups of roughly the same age or configuration)

pick *in* bring in (one picks in the washing from the clothes line)

'Us keeps **pickin'** (picking) 'We keep on going','We carry on somehow'

'Er laffed like a **pisky'**'he laughed maliciously' (like a pixy)

pity *hole* grave

'Tiz like workin wi a busted **prangstick'** literally, 'Like working with a hayfork with a broken handle' – working under great

difficulty

proper good, excellent, *'That's proper'. 'Proper job'* – 'That will do nicely, thank you'.

'Where did ee go to **pub?'** 'Which pub did you go to?'

'They aven't **punished** *ee too much then!'* 'You look very well despite what they [the doctors] have done!' (said to someone after a major operation)

R

''Er's a proper **riptackle'** 'She [a little girl] is a real tomboy'. The word dates from the days of horse-drawn implements when a badly broken horse would rip the harness (tackle) to pieces

S

Give him fair **scope** give someone the benefit of the doubt (perhaps unwisely), give someone too much room for manoeuvre in ques-tionable circumstances

mad (or wild) as a **scot** very angry, fierce

several really rather a lot

'There was several volk up Churchyard'

Sick unwell *'Ow be'ee then? Silly question I s'pose, you'm sick, you wouldn't be yur else!'* (Often overhead in a surgery)

sidling *ground* steep ground, which is difficult to cultivate

spaiks [speaks] **of rain** 'It looks like rain.' We may now rely on the Radio or TV weatherman, but in earlier days one would hear *'Spaiks ov rain you, leaves be turnin' up'*.

stag a cock bird among hens

sticks logs, tree trunks (see *firelights*)

swettin straims perspiring very freely

T

teddy *fat weather* damp warm weather which makes potatoes grow fat

telephone *English* speaking consciously without use of accent, idiom, or dialect. Many country people virtually speak two languages, their natural dialect amongst themselves and a language reserved for communicating with 'foreigners' (on the telephone especially)

telling speaking *'Wot be telling bout?'*

terrify, terrification teasing *'I do like to terrify they boys'*

thunder and lightning bread spread with golden syrup and cream

ticket bill, invoice, any important bit of paper

times often, frequently *'I've telled ee times'*

toad person, usually with overtones of pity or dislike *'Poor ol toad', 'zum careless toad', 'zilly ol toad'*

'Us must get off whoam, us'll get **tongue** *pie else!'* Tongue pie – a scolding, a nagging

travel to move across the ground *'Tis too wetty ter travel'*

travelling visiting (surreptitiously) *'Er's travellin ni' dimes'*, said of a married woman believed to be visiting a lover

two-to-once dealing with

more than one matter at
a time

U

'Er's gone up *shop'* one
generally goes *'up shop'*
or *'up our Emily's'*

upright *twelve* midday
(or midnight), exactly
on the hour (upright
four, five, six, etc.)

keep upsides *with* keep
up with, be as good as

V

valiant agressive

viddle fiddle (violin), an
implement for sowing
grass seed

'Gid vore *roun, dug!'* an
order given to a cattle
or sheep dog to get
round in front of the
flock or herd. *'You
can't have two
vorenoons in one day'*
reply to a man who said
that he was 'feeling his
age'

W

'She'm a bit wapsie *today
like!'* She (the
speaker's wife) is a bit
cross today. A *wapsie* is
a wasp

every whip *and trip, every*
whips *while* every now
and again

Whitsunday stitchwort
(flower)

*'I thought I knawed ye
when I seed ye, but I
couldn't call ye
whoam'* 'I thought that
I recognised you but
couldn't remember
where we had met'

wicked angry *'I feel
propper wicked!'*

*The grass in that there
field's so thick's a* wig

workish *weather* usually
in negative form: *'Baint
workish weather, you!'*
Too hot, or too pleasant
to go to work

made wise pretended, put
on an act

Y

*'I've had a tarrible bad
yurole* [ear-hole] *an it
lodged in me neck'*
(the speaker had swollen
glands in her neck
caused by inflammation
in her ear.)

Z

baint zackly not exactly
right (in the head)

zeem-zo seems to be the
case *'They'm zellin
varm, zeem-zo'*

5

DIALECT WORDS

IN 1839 *A Devonshire Dialogue in Four Parts* was published. This little book contains a glossary prepared by the Reverend John Phillips which sets out to explain the meaning of the dialect words used in the book. It is a record of conversations between a servant maid called Betty and her lover Robin. It is a simple and pleasant story, refreshing in its innocence, but the most interesting thing about it is not the story or what is contained in the glossary, but what words have been left out.

Whereas many of the words used in the text are carefully explained, even more words which would now certainly be regarded as dialect are ignored by the editor and are not explained at all. This could be due to inefficient editing, but it is much more likely that such words were in common use in the eighteenth century and were not then regarded as being dialect. This led me to wonder how many of our Devon dialect words I could find in the OED. The search took a long time, principally because of the difficulty of knowing how the word might be spelled. It is frequently impossible to determine with any accuracy even the initial letter of the word or to know, for example, whether the word was originally spelled with a V or an F.

Nevertheless I have succeeded in finding quite a lot of words, although many are said to be obsolete. When I have found a word in its original form, or an obviously related root word, I have shown in brackets the approximate date of its first appearance in writing. This of course in no way fixes the antiquity of the word itself, and one can be certain that it was spoken for many years before it was first written.

51

Some of the words that I have listed are obsolescent if not yet obsolete, others are rarely used and are probably known only to a few dialect speakers, but I have included them because, in my experience, having seen a word in an old publication, one quite frequently then hears it used in conversation or *vice versa*. An example of this occurred in the early 1970s. One of our neighbours was an old lady who spent the winter huddled over the fire in her front parlour, seldom appearing in public between October and May. I was therefore surprised one bitterly cold January afternoon to see her at her front door. When I asked what she was doing out on such a beastly day, she replied *'Tiz gwain ter blunk,'* and she pointed to the leaden sky. Clearly she meant that it was going to snow, but I had never before heard the word. I asked many local people if they had, but the answer was always the same. I could find nobody who had! I gave up, and thought that I had misheard her until I eventually found the word in Mr Phillips' glossary. It seems that one can have a *blunk ov znaw* or a *blunk ov vire*, a snowflake or a speck of burnt material, which looks something like a snowflake, rising from a fire. Since I found that word and the related word *blunkin* in writing, I have heard it several times in casual conversation.

In this section I deal only with definitions and historical origins and not with etymology. This is because while in my opinion a word can only be enjoyed to the full if one knows its etymology, sometimes a translation is all that is immediately required by the reader. The etymology of dialect words is covered in the final sections of this book.

VOCABULARY

Dialect Words

A

abew (aboue, *c.*1596) above

addle-gutter (adelan, *c.*1000) stagnant gutter or pool

adrowed (adruwode, *c*.1000) dried

agenst to meet *'go agenst Feyther'*

aggets (agats – precious striped stones, *c*.1570) marbles

ail (*c*.1000) awn (beard) of barley

ailer, hailer (heale – a secret place, *c*.897, hale – a tent *c*.1330) tarpaulin, rick cover, horse blanket, someone who conceals a crime or misdemeanour – *'The ailer's so bad as the stailer'* – the person who conceals a theft is as bad as the person who steals

ale-up (halen – to pull up, *c*.992) to pull up earth around growing plants, particularly potatoes *'us'll ale-up they teddies'*

allen summer good, fine summer

allow (*c*.1548) to come to a conclusion *'I allow you'm right'*

aneest (anend, *c*.1325) close to, nearby, nigh

angledog, angletwitch (angeltwaeccean, *c*.940) common earthworm

appledrain, appledrone (OED, but no date given) wasp

aps abcess

arrants article carried when running an errand (not the errand itself)

arrish (edisc, *c*.700) stubble, what is left in the field after corn has been cut and carried, the after-math of a crop

arrish mooey, arrish-mow (see *mow* and *mooey*) small temporary ricks made of stooks of corn stacked on top of each other to allow rain to drain off when the weather is wet and the corn not yet fit to carry – see also *gook*

auncy anticipate bad tidings, be apprehensive

auvis eaves of a building

avore before

axen (aescean, *c*.1000) ashes

axwaddle to wallow on the ground

axwaddler originally a lowly person who went around farms buying ashes to sell to soap

makers, now a term of
disdain or reproach

B

bap (bappis, *c*.1513)
small loaves of bread.
This word is not
confined to Devonshire.
See *cut-rounds*

bar-ire (see ire) crow-bar

barleyzears awns of
barley

bawked something,
somebody that is thrust
forward

bay-spittle honey

beastings (beost, *c*.1000)
colostrum, the first milk
from a newly-calved
cow

beaufet (OED, no date) a
glass-fronted display
cupboard

begayed bewitched

belve (belwe, *c*.1305) to
bellow or shout, sing
loudly *'I do like a hymn
wot I can belve out!'*

ben (ben – the inner part,
14th cent.) the truth of
the matter, the inside
story

biddle to enlarge, to grow
bigger *'They onions be
biddled', 'You'm a
biddle-aided
drumbledrane'* a big-

head (literally, 'you are
a swollen headed
bumblebee')

billers (billure, *c*.1440)
hollow stems of
umbelliferous plants
such as cow parsley

billery to be hollow, like
a *biller*

bird, burd (burde,
c.1300) a form of
endearment, form of
address between persons
of either sex *'Mornin
my burd!'*

bissle to make dirty, to be
dirty. Said to a grubby
little four-year-old: *'Mr
Downes doan't like
bissle lill maids like
you'*

bist (*c*.1000) you are, are
you? *'Thou bist a
prapper vule!' 'Bist
gwain up shop?'*

biver (beofian – to
tremble *c*.888) to shake,
tremble, with cold or
fright

bizzy-milk colostrum

blackaid tadpole

blackdrish blackbird

blacktail stoat

bladders blisters

blake (blakien, *c*.1579) to
turn pale, *'Er blaked*

away' – 'he fainted'

blake wi laffin to laugh until one cries

blinemares nonsense

bline-mop blindfold

bloath pecker tom-tit

blooth, bloath (blooth, *c.*1602) bloom, blossom

blunk ov vire spark or fleck of burnt material

blunk ov znaw snowflake

blunkin snowing

bodley any cooking stove, irrespective of its make (Mr George Bodley of Exeter invented a patent cooking stove in 1802)

bowerly handsome, large

brinded fierce (usually animal)

brist fine dust

brit bruised

brither (*c.*1300) brother

brithernlaw brother-in -law

buddled suffocated

buldery, buldering sultry weather

butt (*c.*1796) two-wheeled cart, the body of which is capable of being tipped, used for carrying dung, mangolds, potatoes, often called a *dung-butt*. Also beehive. In old books

I have seen the word used to mean suddenly, but I have never heard it used in this context.

C

caal think *'What do ee caal you'm doing?'*

cabby, cabin mollycoddling *'Er's gone cabby'* – 'He's given in [to someone]'

canker berry (cankers, *c.*1582) berry (hip) of the dog-rose

canker-row wild rose, dog-rose

cannel teening candle light

care (*c.*1849) mountain ash tree

cater cousins (*c.*1547) intimate friends

cauch mixture, nasty mess

chad, chag gorse

chattermag person given to gossip *'Er's a propper ol chattermag!'*

chauk jackdaw

chibbles (chibboles, *c.*1362) spring onions, immature shallots eaten raw in place of spring onions, or in a *'chibble pasty'*

chinkin grass the first

flush of spring grass

chitterlings (cheter-lingis, *c.*1280) pigs' intestines cooked for human consumption. Also human intestines *'I b'aint zackly right in me chitterlings, Doctor!'*

chonchables icicles

chuggypig woodlouse (North Devon), the smallest pig in the litter, *chuggypigs*, a collection of small pigs (South Devon). See also *zowpeg* and *nissledraft*

chur hurry, speed

chyney (cheney, *c.*1634) things made of china

cladgy (cledgie – sticky, cladgy – clogged, *c.*1577) of a waxy consistency (one has *cladgy* varieties of potatoes)

clag, cleg (cleg, *c.*1449) horsefly

claps (*c.*1450) clasp on clothing, door, harness *'Please to ondo this yer claps'*

clauvell (clavel, *c.*1602) beam of wood over a fire-place

clegged, clagged (claggye, *c.*1570) used to describe the condition of an animal whose hair or wool is covered with dried dung

cloam (clame, *c.*1000) clay used for making something

cloamen something made of clay

close (clos, *c.*1489) enclosure (a word frequently used in field names) East *close,* South *close,* Church *close*

clump thump, hit *'Git un a clump roun' the yur-ole!'*

cob (*c.*1602) building material consisting of mud, clay, straw, bracken, sometimes horsehair, and small stones

coin (coynston, *c.*1350) corner of building or wall, corner stone

condiddled (*c.*1746) wasted, spent unwisely

confloption muddle, mixture *'That there's a master confloption, no mistake', 'Tis an ol confloption me Missus makes fer me dinner'*

confuddled confused

coochy left-handed

coose iron tips on toes of hobnail boots *'Take they boots to the cobbler fer coosin an heelin'*, 'coarse', rough, un- pleasant

copperfinch cock chaffinch

courtledge (curtillag, *c*.1206) farmyard

cowflop foxglove

crackety, cracky-wran wren

crams (crams – to fill with false information, *c*.1794) statements that lack credibility, lies (see *A Parcel of ol' crams* by Jan Stewer)

crazed (crased – to break down in health, *c*.1476) painful, sore, hoarse, aching *'I be crazed all auver Doctor!'*

creem (*c*.1746) to squeeze

croosle gossip, to talk confidentially with malice *'They ol' women was croosling together'*

crumpetty crooked, awkward, uncomfortable *'This yer arthur-itis do make me lie abed all crumpetty-like'*

cubbert (*c*.1663) cupboard

culver (culfran, *c*.825) pigeon, dove

curious (curious – full of care, careful, *c*.1386) careful *'I were uncommon curious about that job'*

cut-round soft bread roll, usually associated with cream teas (see also *bap*)

D

dabby nervous disposition *'Er's dabby in the aid'*

dane red-haired man

daps plimsolls, cheap canvas shoes

dashel thistle, *milky- dashels* are sow thistles

datty (see *doany*) hay which is too damp to carry

daver (rhymes with waver *c*.1621) to wither

davery-topped plants or flowers that have wilted *'They lettuces be all davery topped. B'aint vit fer ait!'*

dawkawk, dawbake stupid person *'You'm a gurt dawkawk!'*

deave nits nuts in which the kernels have dried and are inedible (*deave* = deaf, hollow, empty, unproductive, plus *nits* = nuts)

deeve (deaf, *c*.897) corn with shed grain, deaf

dew snail (dewe snayle, *c*.1548) large black slug

diddyman small or insignificant person

dimity, dimmit, dimps, dimpsie (dimmit *c*.1746) twilight, dusk, evening time

discloose bad language

doaney (see *datty*) something (usually grass or hay) that is damp with the morning dew

doilish (doiled, doilt, doillit, *c*.1513) silly, foolish, particularly applied to elderly people *'Poor old toad, er's gettin doilish!'*

dowel (deuel, *c*.1290) the devil

drade, trade (*c*.1697) material, substance, almost anything tangible, often used in derogatory sense *'I doant think much to this yer drade'* (workman speaking of a cheap pot of paint) *'Us be gwain ter ave zum of this yer vallin drade'* (it is going to snow)

drags (draggis, *c*.1388) spike harrows (farm implement)

drangway (drang, *c*.1787) narrow lane, a passageway

dray (dreihen, *c*.1225) pull, draw, carry in cart or trailer *'Us be drayin dung'*, *'Varmer be drayin stones'*. Also used in reference to photography; *'Drayin a photo'* – 'taking a photo'

drecksill, dreckstool doorstep, threshold

drishel thrush (bird)

drumbledrane (*c*.1746) bumblebee

dry-stone ditch (ditch – raised bank, *c*.1568) dry-stone wall (a wall made of stones without the use of cement), a field bank faced with stone

dryth (drythe, *c*.1533) degree of dryness *'There's no dryth in it'* – 'The air is damp'

durn (*c.*1325) a door
frame

durn-aid (head) the cross
piece at top of door
frame, architrave

durndel as above, but
usually applied to trim
around the door frame

dwindle someone with
shoulders hunched with
the cold *'I be rumped
up like a dwindle!'* (A
dwindle is something
that has shrunk in size
or dwindled away)

E

eaver (*c.*1732) perennial
rye-grass (*Lolium
perenne;* a local strain is
known as *Devon Eaver*),
the flowering heads of
any species of grass, a
grass field gone to seed
and no longer fit to cut
for hay or silage *'That
vield be all eavered you,
baint vit fer nort!'*

eggleberry berry of
hawthorn tree

er him, he, it

evil (evall, *c.*1642) fork

F

fancical* (*c.*1671) tasteful,
critical, particular as to
the way work is done

ferry, fairy, vairy, vaire
(veir, *c.*1300) weasel
(*c.*1550 – a polecat)
ferret

flair (flare, *c.*1847) layer
of fat in a side of bacon

flibberts small pieces,
smithereens *'Jist then,
the ole mare, er rinned
agin a wackin gurt big
stone, er kicked the trap
ter flibberts, an er
tratted off alone'*
('Tavistock Goosey
Fair', song by C. John
Trythall)

flicket tantrum, show of
temper

flitterings, flittereens
small pieces (see
flibberts)

floppy dock foxglove

flummoxed puzzled,
defeated

forestain maintain

fouse *fouse it up* – make
a mess of it

fraped (frapped, *c.*1548)
tied up, bound up
tightly, cut back *'Us'll
frape un off, you!'*(of an

---

* Almost any word beginning with F can be pronounced as if it
began with V.

overgrown hedge)

frawzey celebration, party, treat *'Us'll have a propper frawzey, ter zelebrate'*

french nuts walnuts

fuzzchat stonechat

G

gaiked (somebody or something) standing in the way

galley (gally, *c.*1660) frighten, alarm *'Did er galley you Missus?'*

gambers (gamba, *c.*1607) human ankles, hocks of an animal, the joint in the hind leg of a quadruped between the true knee and the fetlock

geddout! expression of surprise or incredulity: Really! Not likely! *'Geddout, you'm pullin me laig!'*

gee (the G is hard, as in give) give

genst (hard G) by the time something is finished *'Genst er vinished talkin'*

glassen object made of glass

glinney guinea fowl

glint peep, look shyly

'Come on een! Doan ee stan there glintin roun' the cornder!'

glousing glowering

goil (goyle, *c.*1617) a ditch or gulley

golden gladdi, gladdy (*c.*1859) yellow-hammer

goocoos bluebells

gook small temporary rick built on stubble during bad weather (see *arish mowey*)

grab (grabbe, *c.*1578) crab apple

granfer grig a long-legged water insect

granfer longlaigs crane fly, daddy-long-legs

greybird thrush (bird)

gridley granular in texture, gritty

grizzle to show the teeth, to grin, to laugh mockingly, also one's face *'mind that branch don't hit ye in the grizzle'*

grockle visitor, holidaymaker (this unpleasing word, of unknown origin, is believed to be a relative newcomer. It is widely used in North Devon, is normally derogatory and

equates to *emmet* (ant),
which is what
Cornishmen call
unwelcome holiday
visitors

grubbish hungry

gulch (gulcheo, *c.*1225)
to gulp greedily, to
swallow

gutsing greedy

gyte trick, habit

H

haler (see ailer) tarpaulin,
rick cover, horse blanket

harnzee heron

havage (*c.*1846) ancestry,
family background *'Er
commeth of good
havage'*

have (rhymes with shave)
(havoir, *c.*1400) behave,
usually in the negative
*'This yer thing bain't
bein have'*

heft (*c.*1558) weigh,
weight *'I heft un in me
'and, twere bout pound
en arf'*

heller wild person,
naughty child *'Our
Will's a proper little
heller!'* – the speaker
may be rather proud of
the child, and implies
that he is a 'chip off the
old block'. *'Er's a*

proper heller, you!' –
the person spoken of is
disreputable. *'Tis a
proper heller, you!'* –
used in conversation
about bad weather,
politics, a break-down
of machinery, or any
other misfortune

hicketty a wooden latch
on one side of a door,
operated by lifting it out
of, or lowering it into its
wooden 'catch'. If one
is on the opposite side
of the door one has to
put one's finger through
a hole bored in the door
to lift the *hicketty*

hickymal titmouse

hogs (*c.*1340) yearling
sheep

homescreech missel-
thrush

hoop bullfinch

hornywink lapwing. At
Hartland, in North
Devon known as
Braddery (Bradworthy)
Hornywink and at
Coombe Martin as a
Challacombe Hornywink

horse-long-cripple
dragonfly

hyvers (rhymes with
divers) an exclamation

'My hyvers!', alternative to 'My dear soul!' or 'Bless me!' Literal meaning obscure

I

ile (ezle, *c.*1000) a beard or awn of barley

ire (15th cent.) iron (see *bar ire*)

item thing, subject under discussion, *'Wot stupid item be on upon now then?'*

J

jabber the lower lip of a fish

jonnick true, truly. If something is unreasonable, untrue, or unacceptable *'T'isn't jonnick you, t'isn't jonnick!'*

K

kaky sticky

kickshaw (17th cent.) amusement, exhibition, entertainment

kracketty wren (bird)

L

lacer, laceing huge *'Tiz a gurt lacer!' 'Tiz a laceing gurt thing'*

lade (load *c.*1502, fixture on cart *c.*1686) load, loaded, full, a ladder-like attachment to

cart or trailer designed to increase carrying capacity

larn (*c.*1300) teach

leary (leer, *c.*1250) empty, unladen, hungry. If one ploughs a field one way, one is *leary* on the return journey

leat (*c.*1590) artificial waterway, brook

leer (*c.*1386) flank (of man or beast)

lend-ay (hay) hay made from permanent meadow grass as opposed to hay made from temporary leys

lent rosens, lent lilies wild daffodils (*Narcissus pseudonarcissus L.*)

lern (*c.*1300) teach

lickker something remarkable, either good or bad *'Twas a propper lickker!'*

linney (linny, *c.*1695) lean-to shed. In the old days one always had a 'cart linney', a covered lean-to in which carts were stored when not in use

long-tailed pie long-tailed-tit

louster (a word of many meanings) hard work, graft, *'Them as cain't scheemy must louster'* – (people who cannot use their brains [scheme] must work with their hands.) Also to make a mess, to spread litter around, or to walk with a swagger

M

main (*c*.1632) very much, considerable, powerful

maister (*c*.1300) Mister (Mr), also normal form of address *'Mornin, Maister', 'Where's Maister to?'*

make-vor foreshadow, prophesy *'The wind maketh vor rain!'*

make wise pretend, pretence, a sham

mascall caterpillar of the Cabbage White butterfly

master (pronounced marster) a word of amplification *'They be master small bullocks', 'That be a master great marrow'*

maun, maund (maunde, *c*.1535, mand, *c*.1725) large round wicker basket with handles attached to rim

maunchuss (maun, *c*.1774) huge, great *'a maunchuss gurt bullock'*

mauth moss

mawses, mores (moran, *c*.1000) roots of plants or tree

min (OED, no date) them

mind (mynde, *c*.1377) remember *'I mind well the time that barn was built'*

mizmaze confusion

mole heave mole hill

mommet (mamet, *c*.1494) scarecrow, an expression of disdain about a person *'Giddout, you'm a gurt mommet'*

moor (more, *c*.1441) unproductive farm land, land which has reverted to waste, common land (as in Dartmoor and Exmoor)

moowey, mow, mowhay (muha – a rick, *c*.725) rickyard (see *arrish mooey*)

mort (*c*.1694) a lot *'There's a mort o' volk up Church, and more down pub'*

mortal (*c*.1716) very *'It's mortal cold,*

'I'm a mortal onlucky ol' chap,
'You've niver yerd zich a caze,
   From mornin till night,
   Nort never goeth right,
Tiz enough to draive any man
   mazed' (Trad.)

moundary mildewed

mump-aid (head) stupid person

mun them *'I knawed mun well enough'*

mux muck

mux adrowed dried muck, dust (see *adrowed*)

N

nackin vore getting along, *'Ow be aul ov ee nackin vore then?'*

nammet (nummet, *c.*1847) mid-morning light meal, snack

natlings intestines

niddick (nuddick, *c.*1558) nape of neck

nimpingang whitlow, festering spot on finger

nisseldraft smallest pig in litter, a runt (see *chuggypig*)

nittles, nittals hazel trees

nointed nointed *'He'm deul's nointed* [Devil's annointed]'

O

obbledeoy

(hobble-de-hoy, *c.*1540) term of distain *'Zum obble-de-oy gurol wrote this yer letter!'* (said of a letter from a solicitor's office)

onhale uncover (*see ailer* and *ale-up*)

onwray undress

oodwall the great woodpecker

orts (ortus, *c.*1440) remains of food, remnants, refuse

owdry cloudy

P

paike tardy person *'Er's a proper ol paike'*. Said of people always behindhand: *'They'm prapper paikey, niver gets to morket on time'*

paiken to doddle *'There they wus, paiken along'*

pair o prangs a dung fork (with four prongs) (see *prang*)

paunched, poached (poching, *c.*1600) land made muddy and pitted through over-stocking, ground churned up by feet of animals

paunchin removing entrails of rabbits

peendy musty (in taste or

smell)

pegslooze pig sty

pert feeling well

pick (OED – throw or pitch) pitchfork with two prongs (see *prang)*

pillem, pillum dust .

pimlevoot club foot

pinchfart miserly, niggardly person

pinking ailing, weakly, querulous

pinswill (pinswels, *c.*1591) small abscess or boil

ploo (plew, *c.*1535) plough

ploo-gide (hard G) ropes used as reins on working horses pulling ploughs or other farm implements

pluff unwell

pook (*c.*1718) haycock

popples, popplestones (papolstanas, *c.*1000) pebbles

port important

power (*c.*1660) great number *'You'll zee a power ov volks down to Exeter fer Debn County Shaw'*

powl to race

powler one who races. (There is a length of road near Woolfardis-worthy in North Devon called Powler's Piece. This is the last straight stretch before Cann's Water, from whence the road winds all the way to the village. It was here that horsemen, or *carriage volk* used to race to try to get ahead of the carts going to and from the lime-kilns at Bucks Mills.)

prang (prange, *c.*1502) hay fork with two prongs

prize (*c.*1681) fulcrum *'Us caint find no prize fer the bar-ire'* (a person using a crow bar as a lever to lift something cannot find a fulcrum for it)

pucker (*c.*1741) fuss, commotion

pug (*c.*1865) sea trout

purt sulking, pouting *'Er's purt an won't say nort'*

pusky short of breath

pussyvantin pestering someone by following him about

Q

quarrel (*c.*1447) pane of

glass in a window

quoin (*c.*1532) corner of building or wall, (see *coin*)

R

rabin urdick robin redbreast

raunch vegetable or salad eaten without first being cooked

raymes (rame, *c.*1497) skeleton, remains of something *'Er only left the raymes of that there pie!'*

revel (*c.*1350) annual feast day, merry-making

rigmarole (*c.*1736) much talk or fuss, something too complex to be clearly understood

rory-tory tawdry, loud in colour (usually applied to someone else's dress)

rowdugs (row rhyming with cow) rough, uncouth men

rucky down, crucky down stoop low, bend the knee

S

savise (savey, *c.*1785) know *'Do er want ter savise it?'* – 'Does he want to understand it?'

scarify (scarified, – in medical sense to scratch *c.*1541, to break up ground *c.*1805) to cultivate, scratch or scrape surface of soil to destroy weed. Also to talk angrily to someone *'I did scarify er, I did!'*

scat (*c.*1837) throw, cast, scatter, a scattering, a small amount; *'Scat un abroad'* – throw it about or break it in small pieces, *'Only a lill ol scat ov rain'* – a shower

scat abroad to become bankrupt

scoud to churn up *'They cows got into the gorden an' scoud un up'*

scrawling (*c.*1380) fidgetting, shifting about on one's chair or seat

scriddick scrap, crumb, small amount of anything, a small, almost worthless coin

scrinches crevices, cracks, places difficult to reach (e.g. with a paint brush)

scrud scab formed over a wound

scuffle (*c.*1798) farm implement for breaking

down soil, a cultivator

scummer trouble, problem *'Us ad a propper ol scummer wi' that job'*

scummer fidget

scummer britches fidgety-britches (someone given to fidgeting)

shalder (*c.*1825) common yellow iris or flag

shammicks (shammock, *c.*1808) a poor lean animal

sherramooze shrew mouse

shippen, shippon (scypene, *c.*900) milking shed, a cow house

shocks sheaves of corn set up in a field after reaping

shrammed (shram, *c.*1787) to be cold

shug shy

skew-wiff askew, crooked in construction

skit diarrhoea (especially in calves)

skittery to be afflicted with diarrhoea

slay-roof sloping roof of lean-to building

sloans (slan, *c.*1000) sloe, sloes (fruit of blackthorn tree)

slommick (slammakin, *c.*1785) untidy, slovenly, sloppy, dirty, (usually said of a female)

slooched slouched *'Er were slooched up in the corner'*

slottery sloppy, untidy (*c.*1553) slothful, slovenly

smeech, smitch (smec, *c.*825) smuts, small pieces of burnt material floating in air, smoke (particularly when it is not wanted, as in a room with a smoking chimney or in a garden affected by someone else's bonfire)

snipey weather cold, sharp frost

snoodle to weep, to waddle like a duck

snooky (snoc-piece of land, *c.*1236) odd shaped piece of anything, particularly of a field

sosedi an interjection, *'My senses! sosedi!'* (probably 'so said I', a version of *'I said to her, I said'*)

splits cut-rounds, baps

spuddle (*c.*1630) to move feebly *'Us found the ol cow, spuddlin 'bout on the ground and er couldn't get up'*

spuddlin digging, raking the earth

squat (sqwat, *c.*1300) squashed *'Er trod on un, an squat un all abroad'*

stag fighting cock of less than one year old (*c.*1730), a cock bird among domestic hens

stap stop, visit *'Er's got zum ov they ol' Frenchies* [French people] *stappin wi un'*

stape (*c.*1512) staple for fencing or holding wire

steep (*c.*1742) to layer a hedge (partially to cut through branches and bend them at the cut to remake a worn or damaged hedge)

stent (stynte, *c.*1569) common ground, limit of right of pasturage on common land

stick (stikke, *c.*1386) handle of an implement such as a fork or hoe

sticks logs for burning, no matter how large

stirrage (sterage, *c.*1513) commotion

stooer a mess (e.g. making lots of dust)

stooks an alternative to *shocks*

strabbly thin, scattered

strammer untruth

stroil (*c.*1758) couch grass *(Agropyrens ripens)*, stubble

stromy streaky

stugged stuck, bogged down

succourable (socourabill, *c.*1400) sheltered, affording shelter

suent (suantly, *c.*1547) smooth (in all senses of the word) *'That went down suent!'* – said of something pleasant to eat or drink. *'It doan't run suent like'* – something is not running smoothly

T

taffity (taffeta, *c.*1588) particular, dainty, fussy about food

tailpipe (*c.*1815) to tie a tin-can to somebody else's dog's tail to frighten it off a farm (I know of a farmer who still does this!)

tallet (*c*.1586) loft above
a building

tell (*c*.1864) talk, speak
'Wot be tellin 'bout
you?'

tempt touch *'Doan't ee*
tempt it' – 'don't touch
it'

therle lean, gaunt, *'Er's*
so therle as a
grey'ound' – a poor
sample (e.g. of grain)

thiggy, thicky that,
thiggy rabbut – that
rabbit, *thicky thar* – that
there

thungy tough, doughy,
like putty

tiddly goldfinch gold-
crested wren

tiddly, tiddly tope wren

tight arter close behind,
'I went fust but Mother
cum tight arter'

till sow seed

tilth (tylthe, *c*.1496) soil
broken down to a
degree of fineness
suitable for tilling

titmal, tittymal titmouse

titty-todger wren

tizzick sick, unwell in
chest

toad riddings frogspawn

tomnoddy tadpole *'Er's*
like a tomnoddy, all aid

an no body'

trapse (trappe, *c*.1400)
walk without pleasure,
drag one's feet wearily

trendle, trendow
(trendyllys, *c*.1493)
salting trough, trough
for making dough,
container for food. *'Nort*
in the trendow' –
nothing in the larder, no
food available

trone to put in wind-rows
'The (cut) grass is all
troned up'

tub (*c*.1602) gurnard

tuffs cut-rounds, baps

U

uff auver discuss, talk
over a subject

up auver upstairs

ur he, it (see er and
section on grammar)

V

vady (*c*.1880) damp,
musty *'The grass be too*
vady fer to siddown'

vake rage, passion

veriken raking over the
soil

vit dress meat, prepare it
for cooking

vitch polecat

vitty correct, in good
order

vly-pecked low living,

inferior thing or person

vore-edge, vorrage headland of field, part ploughed last

vores (*c.*1380) furrows

vrape, frape drawn tight, cut down

vrawed frozen

vreach violently

vuzkite kestrel

vuznapper, vuzchat whinchat

vuzzyvurze sweet chestnuts

W

wallage a large quantity '*Us've got wallages of grass*'

wangery soft, flabby

want (wond. *c.*725) mole (animal)

want-heap mole-hill

Way! Stop! Woah! (command to horse or to human)

wester (westra *c.*963) western

wetty damp, wet '*Tiz a bit wetty, you*' (raining hard!)

whippletree draught bar for pair or more of working horses

whistness melancholy

white sundays pheasant's eye narcissi

widder move about in nervous manner

widdywaddy stupidly weak, not to be relied upon

wildego naughty, unruly child

windle (*c.*1674) redwing, fieldfare

winnard heron (this word appears in the OED but it is said to be a local word for a redwing. In parts of Devon, it is a grey heron)

winnet black cat with patch of white on backside

winnicky weak, inferior, small '*If you puts the bull to young yaffers, you'm only gwain ter get a winnicky lill ol' calf, no good for nort*'

wipe (wype, *c.*1550) cut back, slash. '*Us'll wipe un off, you*' – of an overgrown hedge

wished (wish, *c.*1829) unhappy, miserable, pale

wished as a winnard miserable (as a grey

heron looks when
standing, lonely on a river
bank)

woolpackers cumulus
clouds

woppit (whapp, *c.*1440)
box someone's ears *'Er
geed un a woppit roun
yurrole'*

wran (*c.*1450), wranny
wren

wraxling (wraxlode,
*c.*1000) wrestling

Y

yamming jibbering,
jabbering, outcry

yapping talking *'Us ad a
good ol yap together'*,
*'Us musn't stay yer
yappin all day!'*

yark (*c.*1300) prepare,
make ready, make haste

yawing lambing

yawning, yamming
lambing time

yaws ewes

yen throw into *'Yen it up
in the trailer'*

yessling something falling
down (such as one's
trousers); fidgeting

yeth make haste

yeth ounds, zet ounds
phantom pack of great
hounds

yettin heating

yokey yellow, tawny
coloured

yucks hiccoughs

Z

zamzawed tay tea stewed
in the pot

zamzodden, zamsowden
soft, daft, anything
spoiled by being half
cooked or overcooked

zamzoe, zamzod dough
cake

zartybake stupid person

zauney stupid, simple

zog doze *'I be gwain ter
ave a bit of a zog'*

zour crab crab apple

zourzobs sorrel (plant)

zowpeg woodlouse (see
chuggypig)

zuft daft, soft

zugs bog, soft wet ground

6

ETYMOLOGY

THE etymology of a word is its true original form and meaning. Far too many people, including those who should know better, tend to guess at the origins of words and fall into the trap of believing that one word is derived from another merely because it looks or sounds like it.

Having said this, the temptation to guess is almost irresistible. Earlier in this book I have told of the old lady who said that it was going to *blunk*. What is the origin of this word? I cannot find it in the OED and am sorely tempted to guess that it comes from the French *blanc*. On the other hand perhaps it is derived from the old French *blankete*, or indeed from some other word in some other language. I do not know the answer and doubt if I ever shall.

Hunting for the origins of words can become an addiction. The great Eric Partridge was a self-confessed addict of lexicography and John Moore once said that no one with the normal allowance of curiosity could look for a word in a dictionary without being diverted by the sight of another unconnected and unfamiliar word.

It is a pleasant and harmless addiction leading from the etymology of words to the meaning of place names, the origins of surnames and to the derivation of catch-phrases and slang. In the pages which follow I have only attempted to produce the etymology of what I consider to be true dialect words. My information has been obtained from the Compact Edition of the OED. Every effort has been made to ensure accuracy but I must accept full responsibility for any errors or omissions.

The etymology of Standard English words which are

subjected to change by accent or pronunciation has not been included.

In the following list the dialect word is given with its present English meaning in brackets.

VOCABULARY

Dialect Words and their Etymology

A

aneest (close to) The etymology of this word is not positive, either *ANEND* or *ANENT* from an Old English phrase meaning on a level with. See also Old English *NEAH* meaning nigh

angletwitch (earthworm) This is rather nasty! It is a compound word. Old English *ANGUL,* meaning fish hook (only later line or tackle to which the hook was fastened), combined with Old English *TWAECCA* which had the original sense of piercing or transfixing. Hence something that is transfixed on a hook – bait for fishing.

appledrain (wasp) Another compound. *APPLE* combined with Old English *DRAN* meaning drone, male of honey bee or wasp

arrish (corn stubble) A particularly interesting word. Variant of *EDDISH* usually identified with Old English *EDISC* a park or enclosure. The OED says that it is difficult to see how the Old English meaning could have given rise to the modern sense of the word. I do not agree; it is reasonable to relate stubble to an 'enclosed' field because corn could only be grown successfully in a field which protected the crop from straying livestock

auvis (eaves of a building) Middle Low German *OVESE,* meaning eaves

axen (ashes) axwaddler
Old English *ASCE,* Old
Norse *ASKA*

B

beastings (colostrum) Old
English *BEOST.* Old
High German, *BIOST;*
the first milk drawn
from a mammal,
especially a cow after
parturition

beaufet (sideboard,
cupboard) One of the
words which shows how
unwise it is to guess.
One might (reasonably)
imagine that it has
something to do with
good food. Not a bit of
it! Middle French and
Middle English
BUFFET, meaning a
slap or blow.
Diminutive of Old
French *BUFFE* (modern
French *BAFFE*), a blow.
Partridge records that
Bloch and Wartburg in
their *Dictionnaire
Etymologique de la
langue Française* say
'Perhaps the word
became the designation
of a piece of furniture
because the latter was
originally furnished with
a board that one could
lower', presumably with
a smart tap or with the
sound of a slap

belve (bellow) Middle
English *BELWEN.* Old
English *BELLAN.*
Related to *BELCH* and
BELL

ben (the truth) Middle
English *BINNE.* Old
English *BINNAN,*
within, towards the
inner part; by suggestion
'close to the truth of the
matter'

billers (stem of plant)
Believed to be from
Middle English
BILLETTE, a small
round log; Middle
French *BILLART,* a
staff, (hence *billiards,* a
game played with a
staff)

bird (girl) This is an
interesting etymological
roundabout. It is now
considered to be rather
racy to call a young
woman a bird. It was
not always thus. The
word has come about by
metathesis from the Old
English *BRID* and
BREDAN, meaning

nursling, something to cherish and keep warm, the young of either sex. It was once used in poetry to describe any lady but later was reserved only for young maidens, so was once respectable and even romantic, as it still is in dialect. A husband will say to his wife of whatever age *'Come on my bird, tiz time us was gwaine ome'*.

bist (are you, you are, you will be) Old Saxon *BIST* (Gospel according to St Luke, Chap. 23. v.43 (*c*.1000) 'Today thou bist mid me on paridiso'.

bivver (tremble) Old English *BIFAN,* and Old Saxon *BIVON,* to shake or tremble

blake (to faint, to turn pale) Middle English *BLAKE,* shining, pale white, ultimately giving the modern word *bleach*

C

cater cousins (intimate friends) Johnson claimed that *CATER* came from the French *QUATRE* (four) used in the sense of a cousin, four times removed, he said 'from the ridiculousness of calling cousin or relation to so remote a degree'. There appears to be no etymological support for this and the OED suggests that it referred to persons treated as cousins because they were catered for within the household. It is to be found in Shakespeare (Merchant of Venice, ACT II, scene II) but I believe it still to be in use in dialectal speech. It was certainly used in writing in Devon in the early 19th century.

chibbles (spring onions) French *CIBOULE,* and Spanish *CEBOLLA,* a species of onion *(Allium fistulosum)* now rarely grown in England. It seems that the shoots of spring onions or young shallots look like this onion

chitterlings (pig's intestines cooked for human consumption)

Old English, *CWITH,*
womb. Chitterling is
thought to be a distorted
diminutive of this word.
See also German
KUTTELN, tripe

chitterpie (magpie or
human chatterbox)
Onomatopoeic word;
Dutch *KOETEREN* to
jabber plus *PIE* which
has an etymology which
would fill pages. Latin
PICA and
Indo-European *PIK,* to
pierce

chyney (things made of
china material) Possibly
from the *CH'IN* dynasty
(255-206 BC). The
OED says that China is
not a Chinese word, but
is found in Sanskrit
about the time of the
early Christian era, with
modified forms
elsewhere in Asia.
Marco Polo referred to
it as *CHIN* in 1516 and
the material now called
china is thought
originally to have come
from China

cladgy (waxy, sticky)
Danish *KLAG,*
KLAGGE, sticky mud,

clay

clag, cleg (horsefly) Old
Norse *KLEGGI,* modern
Norwegian *KLEGG,*
horsefly

claps (clasp or fasten)
Middle English (by
metathesis) *CLAPSEN,*
also *clap* and *clip,* to fit
together making a noise
in so doing

clauvell (beam over fire-
place) French
CLAVEAU, keystone of
arch, wedge-shaped
lintel of window

**clavel board, clavey
board** (mantelpiece)
see above

clegged, clagged (animals
fouled with their own
dung) see *cladgy*

cloam (pottery clay) Old
English *CLAM,* mud,
clay

close (enclosure) Middle
English from Old
French, *CLOS* and Latin
CLAUSUM, an
enclosure

coin (corner of wall) Old
French *COING,* an
angle or corner, whence
COIGN, wedge, stamp
to mark precious metals
used as money (coins)

coochy (left handed) French *GAUCHE,* meaning left

courtiledge (farmyard) Old French *COURTILLAGE,* little court or garth, piece of ground attached to a dwelling house and forming one enclosure with it, or so regarded by the law. Now spelled curtillage and, outside dialect, mostly a legal term

crams (falsehoods) Old English *CRAMMIAN,* a derivative of *CRUMMEN,* meaning to insert, press or squeeze, to fill by force or compression. It appears to have become a slang word for lies (filling listeners with false information) in the late 1700s

crazed (in pain) Old French *ACRASER,* believed to be of Norse origin (Swedish *KRASA,* to crackle): to break, to be broken, to be broken down in health. Thus, crazy paving is not what it is generally supposed to be (a silly arrangement of stones), but paving made of broken and cracked stones. Similarly a crazy person is not just simple but broken in his mind.

cubbert (cupboard) A combination of two words, Old English *CUPPE,* a drinking vessel and Old Saxon *BORT,* meaning a board, shelf, or trencher. The combination of the two words remained until the eighteenth century when *cubbert* was the common spelling and presumably the normal pronunciation. It survives only in dialect

culver (pigeon) Old English *CULFRE* from Latin *COLUMBA* dove or pigeon

curious (careful) Old French *CURIUS,* a word with many shades of meaning but originally giving care, being careful, studious or attentive. See also Latin *CURA,* anxiety, care, medical care, to cure

D

dew snail (slug) Old English *DEAW,* Old Saxon *DAW,* to flow, run (dew was formerly believed to flow from the heavens), plus Old English *SNAEGL,* snail or slug

dimity, dimmit, dimps, (twilight) Derivatives of Old English *DIM,* obscure, dim, dark

ditch (a bank) Old English *DIC,* which has also given us dyke. It originally meant channel, deep furrow, excavation, but came to mean the earth thrown up as a result of digging the channel

doilish (in one's dotage) Old English *DOL,* dull, stupid, foolish, particularly when such failings were caused by old age

drade (material, substance) Local pronunciation of trade, Old English *TREDAN,* to tramp, to follow a path for the purpose of commerce, thence goods bought or sold, finally any goods or substance

drags (harrows) Old English *DRAGAN,* to trail anything along the ground or on other surface where there is friction or resistance

drangway (narrow lane) Variant of *DRONG,* Old English *RINGAN,* to press, compress (thence a passage-way through which one presses one's way), Modern German *DRINGEN,* to press forward, to penetrate. (Drangway is one of the many words about which guesses have been made – e.g. *a draying way* along which goods are drawn (see *dray*) but this guess is far from the truth)

dray (carry a load) Old English *DRAGAN,* to draw, originally a sled or something for dragging turf, wood, etc. The word draw as in drawing a picture is from the same root in the sense that the pencil is dragged across the paper. It also gives us the action of extracting something, drawing a tooth, drawing water or drawing the dole. In Devonshire we also *dray* a photograph

drecksill (doorstep) a compound word, German, *DRECK,* mud, filth, and Middle English *SYLLE,* the base of a frame

drumbledrane (bumble-bee) another compound. Old English *DUMB* meaning mute or stupid, plus Old English *DRAN,* to resound or boom. The word therefore suggests a lazy insect that makes a loud noise – a little unfair I think to the attractive bumblebee. The etymology of bumblebee is interesting and worth recording in this context. Middle English, *HUMBLE-BEE,* an insect which hums. Nothing to do with being humble

dryth (degree of dryness) Old English *DRYGE,* to be dry

durn (door frame) Old Swedish *DYRNI,*

Norwegian *DYRN,* a door

E

eaver (ryegrass) French *IVRAIE VIVACE,* ryegrass

evil (shovel) Old English *GEAFUL,* a fork. Alternative form is *GIFFEL,* which has become *evil* by local pronunciation. Quite how a fork became a shovel is not clear; possibly any implement used to shove or push

F

fancical (strange) Late Middle English *FANCY,* a contraction of *FANTASY* which comes to us from Old French *FANTASIE* deriving from Latin and Greek words meaning figures of the imagination, phantom

ferry, fairy, vairy, vaire (weasel) Old French *VAIR,* Latin *VARIUS,* partly coloured. Originally fur obtained from a variety of squirrel with a grey back and white belly, much used for trimming

garments (as was
ermine). It seems that
Cinderella's slipper was
not made of glass
(French *verre*) but of fur
(French *vair*), a much
more likely material

fitch (polecat, ferret) Old
English *FISSEL*

frape (tie tightly, cut
down closely) Old
English (*GE*)
FRAEPGIGA, Old
French *FRAPER,* to
strike, to beat, to bind
tightly, to brace the
cords of a drum by
pulling them together

G

galley (frighten) Old
English *A-GAELWAN,*
to alarm

gambers (hocks of
animal, ankles of
human) Old French
GAMBE, the leg of an
animal represented in
heraldic design. See also
Italian *viola da gamba,*
a viola held between the
legs as compared with
the *viola da braccio,* an
instrument held in the
arms. Also modern
French *JAMBE,* leg

glint (peep, look shyly)

Middle English
GLENTEN, meaning to
glance, to turn aside

goil (a ditch or gulley)
Middle English *GOLET,*
throat, Old French
GOULET, GOLE and
GOULE, throat see also
gurgle and *gullet*

golden gladdi
(yellowhammer) Old
English *GLAED,* bright,
joyous

grab (crab apple)
Swedish *SKRABBA,* the
fruit of wild apple tree

gulch (to swallow)
Swedish dialect
GOLKA, German
dialect, *GULKEN,* to
swallow greedily

H

havage (ancestry) The
verb to have derives
through Middle English
HAVEN or *HABBEN*
and Old English
HABBAN, to hold or to
take. The suffix 'age'
comes from Old French
which has numerous
meanings but includes a
collective sense. *Havage*
simply means the
holding of something
collective, such as

ancestry, lineage or parentage

having (behaviour) (rhymes with shaving) French *AVOIR,* to have. 14th and 15th century variants give the sense of behaviour, bearing, manner.

heft (weigh) Old English *HEBBAN,* (via modern English *HEAVE*) to move up, to move along, to lift

hogs (yearling sheep). A very interesting word. Old English *HAGG,* possibly of Celtic origin. The OED suggests that the word may originally have had reference to the age of the beast. The yearling age-group runs through the use of this word when applied to both sheep and pigs.

I

ile (awn) Old English *EGLE* or *EIGLE* original Teutonic *AGLI.* The OED quotes an early version of the Gospel according to St Luke Chap. 6, v.41, which when translated into modern English, reads 'why see'st thou the barley-awn in thy brother's eye?'

ire (iron) Here is a word which has undergone many changes. Old English *IREN* which in Middle English became *IRE.* The etymology is probably Norse. Partridge relates the *ORE* to the Old English *AR* meaning copper, brass, or metal. The Middle English version is retained in Devon dialects and is in daily use in the compound *BAR-IRE* meaning a crow-bar. The expressive *'It was freezin bar-ires'* is used to describe very cold weather

K

kickshaw (useless ornament, pretty trifle) French *QUELQUE CHOSE* shortened to *QUE'QUE CHOSE,* something, a thing-a-me-bob

L

lade (load, ladder-like fixture on cart) Old English *HLAED,* a stack, pile, load. When used in the context of a cart fixture, something which increases the capacity to carry a load. Survives in standard English in the word *LADEN*

leary (empty) Old English *LAERE*, empty

leer (flank of man or beast) Old English *LIRA*, the fleshy part of the body

lern (teach) A fine example of the use of a word in dialect which is now regarded as being incorrect. Old English *LAERAN*, Middle English *LERNEN*, to teach. Etymologically, the word teach means to show or guide, and one learns by being taught. The dialect 'I'll lern ee' meaning 'I will teach you' is not incorrect

linney (lean-to-shed) Old English *HLINIAN*, to lean. A shed or farm building with open front and lean-to roof. Sometimes spelled linhay, but, contrary to some guesswork

etymology, has *nothing* to do with hay

M

main (powerful) Old Norse *MEGN*, strong, powerful

maund (basket) Old English *MAND*, basket made of wicker or some other woven material

mawses, morses (roots of trees or plants) Old English *MORE*, a root of tree

mind (remember) Old English *MUNAN*, to think, to remember

mommet (scarecrow) Old French *MAHUMET*, an idol, (from false medieval notion that the prophet Mohammed was worshipped)

moor (unproductive land) Old English *MOR*, a moor. Akin to Old English *MERSC* a marsh, from Latin *MARE*, the sea

moowey (rickyard) Old English *MUHA*, Old Norse *MUGE*, a swath, stack of hay, a heap of hay or grain in a barn

mort (a lot) Possibly Old Norse *MART*, great, a

great number, but this is not certain. More likely French *MORTIE,* something (so big) that it frightens one to death

mun (them) Old English *MANNIAN,* a person

N

nammet (mid-morning snack) Variation of *NUMMET,* a corruption of *NOON-MEAT*

niddick (nape of neck) Old English *HNECCA*

O

obbledehoy (term of disdain) Middle English *HOBBLE,* to move with clumsy gait

orts (remains of food, refuse) Not in general use until the end of the 16th century, possibly from Dutch *OOR-AETE,* the remains of food, left-overs

P

paunched, poached (land damaged by over-stocking) Related to words *POKE, POACH* and *POACHER,* to thrust or dig out with fingers. Old English *POHHA,* pocket. Modern French *POCHE,* a pocket or pouch. Hence land that is full of pockets of water and mud

pick (pitchfork) Old French *PIC,* English *PIKE,* a foot soldier's weapon. A pitchfork is very like a pike (and indeed was used as such as recently as the 1940s when the LDV, later the Home Guard, initially had no better weapons than pitchforks).

pinswill (a small boil) Etymology uncertain but probably Old English *PINN* a pin, peg, point (a boil or swelling rises to a point). It also feels perhaps like the pricking of a pin

ploo (plough) Old English *PLOH*

pook (haycock) Old English *POCC,* French *POCHE,* a gathering together, a pocket, see *paunched* above. All these words have the same root.

popples (pebbles) An interesting word. Old English *PAPOLSTANAS* probably onomatopoeic

and said to be the noise
made by water running
over stones

power (a number) Middle
English *POER,* mastery
or power. A large
enough number to be
powerful. See modern
mathematical usage, 'x
to the power of three'

prang (hayfork) Middle
English *PRANGE,*
variation of *PRONGE,* a
sharp pain, hence tine of
fork which can inflict
such a pain. Modern
English *PRONG.* (A
prang is a hayfork with
two prongs, but a *pair
of prangs* is a dung fork
with four prongs)

prize (a fulcrum) Old
French *PRISE,* taking,
seizing, capturing.
Connected with modern
English, *APPREHEND.*
Modern English usage
'to prize open'

pug (sea trout)
Etymology uncertain but
word appears to refer to
the size of the fish since
it is also used to
describe an elf, a small
dog, a small lamb and
other small things. A

pug was probably
regarded as a small
salmon, although this is
of course incorrect

pussyvantin (pestering
someone) French
POURSUIVRE meaning
'to follow'

Q

quarrel (pane of glass)
Middle English
QUAREL, a square.
Thus the word relates to
the shape of the pane,
and not to the material
from which it is made

R

rabin urdick (robin
redbreast) *Rabin* is
simply a dialectal form
of Robin, a pet name for
Robert, but *urdick* is
most interesting. *URD* is
'red' having undergone
metathesis, and *dick* was
an early nineteenth
century word for a
leather apron, a
worn-out shirt. Hence a
covering worn to protect
the front of one's dress
during work: Robin red
apron/shirt/dicky/
breast

raymes (skeleton,
remains) Old High

German *RAMA,* modern German *RAHM,* a framework, the bones or skeleton of a human or animal. In dialect it is used in the context of something left over *'Missus give me the raymes of a rabbut pie fer me dinner'.*

revel (merrymaking). (One still speaks of the 'Clovelly Revels', an annual sports-day/fête raising funds for Church and Parish Hall). Old French *REVEL,* a revolt, din, disorder; hence the noise of merry-making

rigmarole (a lot of talk or fuss, a long letter or document) Middle English *RAGEMAN,* a state or Papal document, esp. of an Act passed in 1276 by King Edward I for the hearing of ancient wrongs. This became *RAGMAN,* and *RAGMAN-ROLLS* were deeds written on parchment on which, in 1291 and 1293, Scottish lords and gentlemen swore allegiance to the King of England

S

savise (to know, to understand) French *SAVOIR. SAVEZ VOUS,* 'Do you know?'

scarify (to scratch surface) Middle French *SCARIFIER,* from Latin *SCARIFICARE,* to scratch

scat (scatter, etc.) Middle English *SCATEREN,* to split up, to strew about

scrawling (shifting in one's seat, fidgeting) A form of *CRAWL,* perhaps suggested by *SPRAWL,* Old English *SPREAWLIAN,* to move in ungainly or awkward manner

scuffle (a cultivating implement) Dutch *SCHOFFEL,* a weeding hoe

shippen (a milking shed) Old English *SCYPEN,* a shed

shrammed (to be cold) Old English *SCRIMMAN,* to be paralysed with the cold

sloans (fruit of blackthorn: sloe, sloes) Old English *SLA* (plural *SLAN*) This plural usage

was recorded in the 17th
cent. It is retained in
Devon dialect. I have
never heard it used in
the singular

smeech (smuts, smoke)
Old English *SMEC,*
smoke, dense or thick
vapour

snooky (odd shaped piece
of something) from the
standard English *NOOK,*
Middle English *NOK,* a
nook, corner, angle

squat (squashed) Old
French *ESQUATIR,* to
crush, flatten, beat out
of shape, smash, squash,
bruise

stag (a cock bird) another
word which refers to the
sex of the subject. Old
English *STAGGA,* Old
Norse *STEGGI,* a male
bird. In modern usage, a
male deer

stape (a staple) Old
English *STAPOL,* a
post, pillar, step, a
looped device from
which to hang
merchandise in a market
place. Middle English
ESTAPLE, a mart

steep (to layer a hedge)
Old English *STUPIAN,*

to stoop down, to bow,
hence to bend down
branches of saplings to
make a hedge

stent (common land
boundry) Old French
ESTENTE, meaning
extent - the limitation
on freedom of pasturage
on common land

stick (wooden handle of
hoe or fork) Old English
STICCA, to pierce, a
pointed instrument, a
rod with which to pierce
or poke, a piece of
wood shaped for a
purpose

stirrage (commotion) Old
English *STYRIAN,* to
disturb

succourable (sheltered)
Old French
SO-SUCURABLE,
affording succour,
helpful. Modern French
SECOURS, relief, aid

suent (smooth) Old
French *SUIANT,* modern
French *SUIVRE,* to
follow, thus to proceed
smoothly, evenly

T

taffity (dainty) Old
French *TAFFETAS,*
silken cloth, hence

something attractive, dainty

tallet (a loft) French *TABULARE,* floor-boarding. (A tallet is a loft formed by laying boards over the rafters of a cattle shed or stable)

tell (talk, speak) Old English *TELLAN,* what one has to tell, to talk about

tellan (speaking) see above. 'I doan't knaw wot you be tellan bout!'

tempt (to touch) Middle English *TEMPTEN* from Latin *TEMPTARE,* to touch

tilth (soil sufficiently broken down for sowing seed) Old English *EORTHTILTH,* labour involved in cultivation, tillage, husbandry

trendle (salting trough) Old English *TRENDEL,* a circle or ring, a vessel of flat and rounded form, a circular trough or tray used by bakers

V

vores (furrows) Old English *FURH,* Middle Dutch *VOOR,* a narrow trench made in the earth for drainage purposes, or to receive seed at planting time

W

want (mole) Old English *WAND* or *WOND,* mole or shrew

wester (western) Old English *WESTRA,* lying towards the west

wipe (to cut or slash) Old English *WIPIAN,* to wind around, to whip, to slash

wran (wren) Old English *WRENNA* or *WERNA*

wraxling, wrassling (wrestling) Old English *WRAXLIAN,* to wrestle, strive, contend

Y

yamming (jibbering) Middle Dutch *JAMMER* (pronounced yammer) a loud outcry

yark (to make ready) Old English *GEARCIAN,* to prepare, make ready

7

ENGLISH-DIALECT VOCABULARY

THIS vocabulary consists of standard English words and their equivalents in local pronunciation or in dialect.

A
abscess aps, pinswill
about bouta
above abew, up auver
account counton
afraid aveered, feared, veered
after arter
after all avore-aull
against agin, genst, gin, ginst (hard g)
ailing pinking
alder (tree) aller
Alfie, Alfred Aufy, Offy
Alice Else
alight (from something) onlight
alms ormers
always awiz, orwiz
amazed maized, mazed
am not ant
ancestry havage
andiron viredog
angle ango
angle-iron ango-ire

ankles gambers
anointed nointed
another anither
anxious angshus
anything aut, awt
apron apern
argue argify, argy
ashes axen
ask ax
asked axed
attacked attack-ted
audacious owdacious
aught ort
awkward ockard
awn ile, barleyzears (awn of barley)
B
baby babby
baby boy biye
baby girl cheel
back-kitchen backouze, back-house
backwards assards, backsivore
bankrupt (to become), go

scat, go squat
bark (like small dog) yap
barley awns barleyzears
barrel barriole
bawl baal
beam (over fireplace)
  clauvel
bean bain
beastly bissle
beasts baistzez
beautiful britiful, bootiful
beauty booty
because cos, cuz,
  vor-why
bed baid
beef baive, beeve
been bain, bin
beer bair
beetle biddle
before avore, be-vower,
  vaur, vor
before daylight vaurday
behave being-have
  (rhymes with shave)
bellow belve
bellows bellerziz
belly-band bellybon
bequest bequath
besides azides
bewitched begayed
bigoted bigotive
bird baird, bard, burd
biscuit bisky
blackbird blackdrish
bleed blaid
blindfold bline-mop

blisters bladders
blood blid
bloom bloath, bloo,
  blooth
blossom blooth
bluebells goocoos
bogged down stugged
bogs zugs
boil bile
boiling bile-in
borrow borry
bottle boddle
boy biye, bye
brambles brimbles,
  brimmels
bread braid
breakfast braxis, braxus,
  brexis
breeches burches
bridge burge
bronchitis brantitis,
  brown-titus
brook (artificial) leat
brother brither
brother-in-law
  britherernlaw
bruised brit
brush brish
bull bool, bule
bullfinch hoop
bumblebee drumbledrane,
  umble
burst bost, bust
business bizzens
butchering butchin
by-and-by bimeby

C

candle cannel
candlelight cannel
  teening
cannot cas'n
careful curious
carpenter cafender
cart (carry) dray
case cause, caze
cast (scatter) scat
cat (female) yaw-cat
catch ketch
caterpillar (Cabbage
  White) mascall
celebration frawzey
certain zartain
chaffinch (cockbird only)
  copperfinch
challenge channis
chamber chimber
cheek chack
chestnuts (sweet)
  vuzzyvurze
child cheel
chimney chimbley,
  chimley
china (material) chyney
chit chid
chore chewer
clasp claps
clay (object made of clay)
  cloam, cloamen
clerk clurk
clever cliver
climb climey
clod clat

close (to, by) tight-arter
clothes claws
cloudy owdry
clover-hay cloveray
club-foot pimple-voot
coarse coose
coat caw-at
cock bird stag
cold (to be) shrammed
collection (of something)
  passel
colostrum beastings,
  bizzy-milk
comfortable con-for-able
common-ground stent
commotion stirrage
confused confuddled
confusion mizmaze
consequence konekense
contemptible shitten
continue continny
cor! (exclamation) gaw!
corner coin, cornder,
  (corner of building,
  wall), quoin
correct cracked, krackt
couch grass stroil
crab apple grab
cranefly (daddy-long-
  legs) granfer-longlaigs
creak crake
cream craim
crooked crumpetty
crop crap
crow-bar bar-ire
crumb crub

cultivate (the soil) scarify
cupboard cubbert
cupboard (glass-fronted) beaufet
curlygreens (vegetable) crilly-grains
cut (back, down) frape, vrape, wipe-off

D

daffodils (wild) lent lilies, lenten roses
daft mazed, zamsowden, zamzodden, zuft
dainty taffity
damp vady
dandruff scruff
daren't durzant
daughter darter
dead daid
deaf deef, deave
deal (wood) dell
dearly dairly
deceit dezait
deceive dezaive
delay hinderment
depth deepth
devil dowell
Devon Dabn, Debn, Demshur
diarrhoea (esp. in animals) skit
die dee
directly drackly
dirty bissle, shitten
discuss uff auver
doesn't dith'n, doth'n

dog dug
done, did dood
don't know dannaw, disn't naw
doorframe durn, durnaid, durndle
doorstep, threshold drecksill, dreckstool, druckstool
dotage doilish
doze zog
dragonfly horse-long-cripple
draw (carry, cart, take) dray
dried adrowed
drive draive, draw
drove drauved
dust brist, mux-adrowed, pillum
duster dister

E

each aich
ear yer, yur, yurole
earth ay-uth
earthworm angletwitch, angletwitch
eastern easter
easy aizy
eat ait, ate
eel ail
eggs aigs
either aither
elephant huffilant
eleven lebn, lem
else alse, ulse

empty empt (to empty)
  leary (to be empty)
end aend, ayend
engine injin
enough nuff
entertainment
  intertainment
equal aikel
errand arrant
eternal tarnal
evening ayve-mun,
  aivmin, evelings
ewe yaw
exactly zackly
F
faith feth, fey
fall vahl, vall
far var
farmer varmer
farming varmering
farm-yard curtiledge
farther varder
farthest vardist
fast vast
fault vot
features (looks) vaityers
fen venn
ferret fitch
fieldfare windle
fierce brinded
fire avire
fire-dog viredug
fish vish
fit, fitting vitty
flabby wangery
flank leer

floorboards planchin
fool vule
forewarning voretoken
foxglove cowflop,
  floppy-dock
frighten frit, galley
frightened aveered
frogspawn toadriddings
from vrim
front furnt
frozen vrawed
furrows vores
furze vuzz
fuss (commotion) pucker,
  stirrage
G
gate ge-at
gate hook (fastening to
  gate) ge-at ook
getting along, getting on
  nackin vore
giggle siggle
gin jean
girl (baby) cheel
give gee
glance (peep) glint
glass (something made of)
  glassen
glowering glousing
goes goeth, go'th
going gain, gwain
goose guze
gooseberry goosegog
gorse chad, chag, fuzz,
  vuzz
gossip croosle

guinea-fowl glinney
gulley goil
gurnard (fish) tub
grandfather gonmer,
 granfer, grampy
grandmother gonmer,
 grammar
gravel grovel
greased graized
great (large) gurt, master,
 maunchuss
greedy gutsing
green grin
H
habit (conduct) gyte
hair ayer
halfpenny apmee
hames aimzes
handkerchief ankcher
handsome ansum,
 bowerly
happen apn
harken arken
harrows (spike) drags
hasp apse
haste (make haste) yeth
haul all
have hab
have not abn, habn
hawk (any bird of prey)
 kit
haycock pook
hazel bushes nittals
he er, ur, ee
head aid

headland (of field)
 vore-edge, vorrage
hear yur
heat yet
heath yeth
heating yettin
heave ay-ve
heifer yaffer
heinous hengous
hedge ay-je
hedgehog ay-je-boar
hedge trough (ditch)
 ay-je-draw
herbs arbs, yarbs
here yur, yer
heron harnzee, winnard
hey-ho! hey-go!
hiccough yucks
hill eel
hindrance hinderment
hit clump, dap
hoard wurd
hocks gambers
hold holt
holiday-maker grockle
holler holley
honey bay-spittal
hook ook
hope awp, awps
horsefly clag, cleg
however owsom-iver
huge laceing, maunchuss
hungry grubbish, leery,
 ungered
hurry chur
hurt orted

I
icicles chonchables
idiot idjit
ignorant iggerant
impertinence himperence
impossible onpossible
improper onproper
impudence himperence
in een
indecency ondaicentness
indecent ondaicent
inferior (in size)
    winnicky
inflammation infermation
injured orted
interfere (meddle) meel
intestines natlings
inwards (inward parts)
    innards
iron ire
irregular onwriggler
J
jackdaw chauk
jolt jolk
judge jidge
jumble-sale jumbo-zale
K
kale caul
kestrel vuzkite
key kay
kite kit
knew nawed
knocked nacked
know savis
L
laden lade

lapwing hornywink
large bowerly, gurt,
    hengous, laceing
    (something large – a
    lacer)
later bimeby
lath (as in lath and
    plaster) laff
laughed laffed
launch laanch
lean lain, therle
learn larn
leave laive
lee (sheltered from wind)
    lew, loo
leg laig
listen arken
litter (rubbish) louster
little leel, leet
load law
loan lent
loft tallet
logs sticks
look! (see!) lookee!
losing losting
lover luvver
M
maintain forestain
man mun
marbles aggets, marvels
market margit, morket
marshes mashes, moors
masonry (working as a
    mason) masony
master maister
mattock doobail, fisgie,

maddock
mean nair
meddle meel
melancholy whistness
mice meeze
might (power) me-art
mildewed moundary
milk (to milk) mulkee
miserable wisht
missel-thrush
homescreech
mole want
molehill mole heave,
want heap, want heave
monkey mokus
moor (wet, unproductive
land) ma-ur
morning vorenoon
moss mauth, mose
mould moulder
muck mux
mucky, muddy muxy
mushroom mushelroom
musty peendy
N
nape of neck niddick
naught nort
naughts and crosses
aughts'n crosses
naughty child lill heller,
wildego
near (mean) nair
neither nother
never niver
none noan
nonsense (to talk n.)

blinemares
northern norther
nose nawse
nothing nort
notice nawtiz
O
oats wuts
officer hossifer
old aud
old woman (wife)
o-dumman
one another one tother
open ope
otherwise else
ought ort
oven omm
over awver
overthrow auverdraw
owned awned
P
package passel
painful crazed
pale blake, pallid, wisht
pane of glass quarrel
panting pankin
parcel passel
parson passen
particular taffity
particularly purtickly
partridge paltridge
party (celebration)
frawzey
passageway (narrow)
drangway
passion (anger) vake
peace paice

pebble popple, popplestone
peep (look shyly) glint
perfection purveckshun
photograph votee
piece paice
pig peg
pigeon culver
pigsty pegslooze
pillow peel
pillowcase peel-bears
pitching (throwing) pitchin
pity pittis
pixy piskie, pisky
planking (floorboards) planchin
plenty hundreds
plot (of land) plat
plough ploo
poison powsen
pole pool
polecat fitch, vitch
poor pawer
polyanthus polyanties
post (stake) pauss
posts posses, postses
potato tater, teddy, tiddy
pour pawer
prepare (make ready) yark
pretend make wise
primrose pimrose, primrosen
print pernt
prong prang

proper prapper, vitty
pull (draw) dray
puzzled flummoxed
Q
quantity (of something) passel
quay kay
queen cat yaw cat
queer qui-ar
quiet kwai-it
R
rage vake
rattle rittle
raw rare
reach raich
red urd
redwing windle
remains orts, rames
remember mind
revel (jollification, fête) rail
ribbons erbons, urbons
rich urch
Richard Urchard
rickyard moowey, mow, mowhay
ridiculous re-dicklus
road raud, rawed
robin redbreast rabin urdick
roots (of tree or plant) mawses, mores
rotted ratted
roughcast rowcast
row raw
royal rile

rubbish rummage
run rin
runt (smallest pig)
  chuggy-pig, nissledraft
rusty risty
rut rout
S
salt zalt
sand zand
sap zap
saucy sassy
scarecrow mommet
scatter scat, zlatter
scheme gyte, scheemy
scholar scollard
scurf scruff
sect sex, zext
sell zill
several sivver
shabby (trick) scabby
shale (sedimentary rock)
  shillet
sheep shape, yaws
shelter (from wind)
  lewness, lewth
sheltered side lewzide,
  succorable
shitty (dirty) shitten
shoot shet
shout holly
shovel evil, shoel, showel
show (exhibition) shaw
shred shreed
shriek scritch
shut shet
shy shug

sick tizzick
sieve zaive
sigh sife, sify
simple-minded zauney
skewer skivver
skin skeen
slam stram
sloe (fruit of blackthorn)
  sloans
smallest smarless
smooth suent
snack (elevenses)
  nammett
sneeze neeze
snowing blunkin
soft (flabby) wangery,
  zamzodden
soil ay-uth
soldier sauger, sodger,
  solger, sudger
something zummat
sooner (rather) zoonder
soul zaw
southern souther
sow (seed) till
speak spake
speckled spekerty
spectacles spurticles
speed chur
squash squat
squat quot, quat
squeeze creem
squeamish skimmish
staple (fastening) stape
started starded
staunch staint

stay bide
sticky kaky, clitchy
stinks stanks
stoat blacktail
stolen stauld
stonechat fuzzchat
stoop steep
stormy (sky) stromy
stove bodley, stauve
streaky stromy
struggling spuddling
stubble arrish
stuck (bogged down)
 stugged
stump stub
stupid stoopid
suffocated buddled
sure zartain, zhure
sun zin
swallow (consume) gulch
swath (of grass) zwar,
 zwaur
sweltering quelstring
T
tadpole blackaid,
 tomnoddy
talk tell
talking yabbing, yappin
tantrum flicket
tap (hit) dap
tarpaulin haler
tasks chewers
tea tay
teach larn
tear (break) tar
tease (wool) toze
tease (annoy) terrify

tedious tayjess
thatching datchin
thaw (to thaw something)
 onthaw
them mun
thin strabbly
thing item
thirteen dirteen
thistle dashel
thrash drash
three dree
throat drot
throw ay-ve, scat
throwing pitchin
thrown drowed, drawed
throw up (vomit, refer
 back) draw-up
thrush (bird) drish,
 drishel, grey-bird
thump clump
tight-fisted nair
titmouse hickymal,
 titmal, tittymal
titter siggle
toad taw'd
tom-tit bloath-pecker
touch tempt
tough thungy
towards genst (hard g)
tread trade
tremble biver
tremendous hengous
trial (in court) yurrin
trick gyte
trough draw, traw, trow
 true jonnick
two doo

U
uncivil ondaicent
uncomfortable
  oncomforable
uncover onhale
understand savis
undress onwray
uneven onwriggler
unknowing onnawin
unpunctual onwriggler
untruth strammer
unwell pluff
upon pun
upset upzot
upstairs up auver
V
value valley
vehicles vay-acles
vermin varmint
veterinary vetinry
victuals vittles
violently vreach
visitor (holidaymaker)
  grockle
W
wager wajer
walk (wearily) traipse
wallowing walvin
walnut frenchnut
warrant waarn
wasp appledrain,
  appledrone, wapsie,
  wopsie
weak wick
weasel ferry, fairy, vaire,
  vairy

weather ware, wur
wedge waj
weigh heft
western wester
whet (sharpen) wad
whinchat vuznapper,
  vuzchat
whitlow nimpingang
wicked nointed
wife wive
William Wi-yum
with way
within way-een
without uthout
woman ooman, dumman
wood ood
woodlouse (North Devon
  dialect) chuggypig
woodpecker oodwall
world ay-uth, wurdle
worm angledog,
  angletwich
would wude
wren crackety,
  cracky-wran, kracketty,
  tiddly tope, titty-todger,
  wran, wranny
wrestling wraxling
Y
yellow (coloured) yokey
yellow-hammer golden
  gladdi, gladdy
yes ace, ees, iss
yourself yerzel
Z
Zed (the letter) zad

INDEX OF DIALECT WORDS

See also English/Dialect Vocabulary

102

BIBLIOGRAPHY

THIS bibliography lists some of the works consulted in dealing with this subject. Publication dates are those of the editions used by the author.

AUSTEN, JANE, *Persuasion* (first published 1818). London; Dent, 1906 Everyman's Library. New York; Dutton, 1906.

BARZUN, JACQUES & GRAFF, HENRY F., *The Modern Researcher*. New York, Chicago, San Francisco, Atlanta; Harcourt, Brace & World Inc., 1970.

BAUGH, ALBERT C. & CABLE, THOMAS, *A History of the English Language*. London; Routledge and Kegan Paul, 1951.

BOWRING, Sir JOHN, *Language with special reference to the Devonshire Dialects*. Report and Transactions of the Devonshire Association, 1866.

CHOPE, R. PEARSE, *The Dialect of Hartland, Devonshire*. London; Kegan Paul, Trench, Trubner, 1891.

COBBETT, WILLIAM, *Rural Rides*. London; J. M. Dent & Sons Ltd, Everyman's Library, 1912, reprinted 1966.

COLES, ALBERT, J., *Ole Biskit*. London; Herbert Jenkins, 1933. *A Parcel of ol' Crams*. Gloucester; Alan Sutton Publishing Limited, 1980. (First published 1930, republished 1980 by arrangement with the copyright holders).

CRYSTAL, DAVID (ed), *Eric Partridge, in His Own Words*. London; André Deutsch, 1980.

DEVONSHIRE ASSOCIATION FOR THE ADVANCEMENT OF SCIENCE LITERATURE AND ART, *Report and Transactions,* 1877. (This particular volume contains the terms of reference of the committee established to record Devonshire provincialisms, and for this reason has been singled out. All annual reports and transactions since that date contain reference to dialect).

EKWALL, EILERT, *The Concise Oxford Dictionary of English Place Names.* Oxford University Press, 1936, 4th edn, 1960.

ELWORTHY, FREDERICK THOMAS, *The Dialect of West Somerset.* London; Trubner, 1875-86. (This volume contains three works, originally presented as individual papers: (i) *'The Dialect of West Somerset',* (ii) *'Grammar of West Somerset Dialect',* and (iii) *'West Somerset Word-Book or Glossary'.*

GWATKIN, Mrs (ed), *A Devonshire Dialogue in Four Parts.* Plymouth; Edward Nettleton, 1839. London; G. B. Whittaker, 1839.

HALLIWELL, JAMES ORCHARD, *Dictionary of Archaisms and Provincialisms.* London; George Routledge and Sons, 1904. New York, E. P. Dutton & Co, 1904.

HEWETT, SARAH, *The Peasant Speech of Devon.* London; Elliott Stock, 1892.

HOLE, The Reverend WILLIAM, *The Exmoor Scolding and Courtship.* London; *The Gentleman's Magazine,* 1746.

JENNINGS, JAMES KNIGHT, *The Dialect of the West Of England.* London; John Russell Smith, 1869.

MARTIN, E. W., *The Secret People.* London; Phoenix House Ltd, 1954. New York; Transatlantic, 1956. *The Shearers and the Shorn,* London; Routledge & Kegan Paul. New York; 1965, Humanities Press, 1965.

McADAM, Jr, E. L. & MILNE, GEORGE, *Johnson's Dictionary, a Modern Selection.* London; Book Club Associates, by arrangement with Victor Gollancz Ltd, 1982.

MOORE, JOHN, *You English Words.* London; Collins, 1961.

ORTON, H. and Others (ed), *Survey of English Dialects* (1961-72). E. J. Arnold. *The Linguistic Atlas of England.* Croom Helm, 1978.

Oxford English Dictionary, Compact Edition. Oxford University Press, 1971, Book Club Associates, 1979. (This is the complete text of the 1933 re-issue, reproduced micrographically, condensing twelve volumes into only two).

PARTRIDGE, ERIC, *A Dictionary of Slang and Unconventional*

English. London; Routledge, 1937. *Usage and Abusage: A Guide to Good English.* New York; Harper, 1942. (1st British edition, revised and enlarged, London; Hamilton, 1947). *Origins: A Short Etymological Dictionary of Modern English.* London; Routledge and Kegan Paul, 1958. *The Gentle Art of Lexicography, as pursued and Experienced by an Addict: A Memoir.* London; André Deutsch, 1963.

PHILLIPS, The Reverend JOHN, *Glossary to the Devonshire Dialogue in Four Parts.* Plymouth; Edward Nettleton, 1839. London; G. B. Whittaker, 1839.

TREVELYAN, G. M., *English Social History.* London; Longmans Green, 1944.